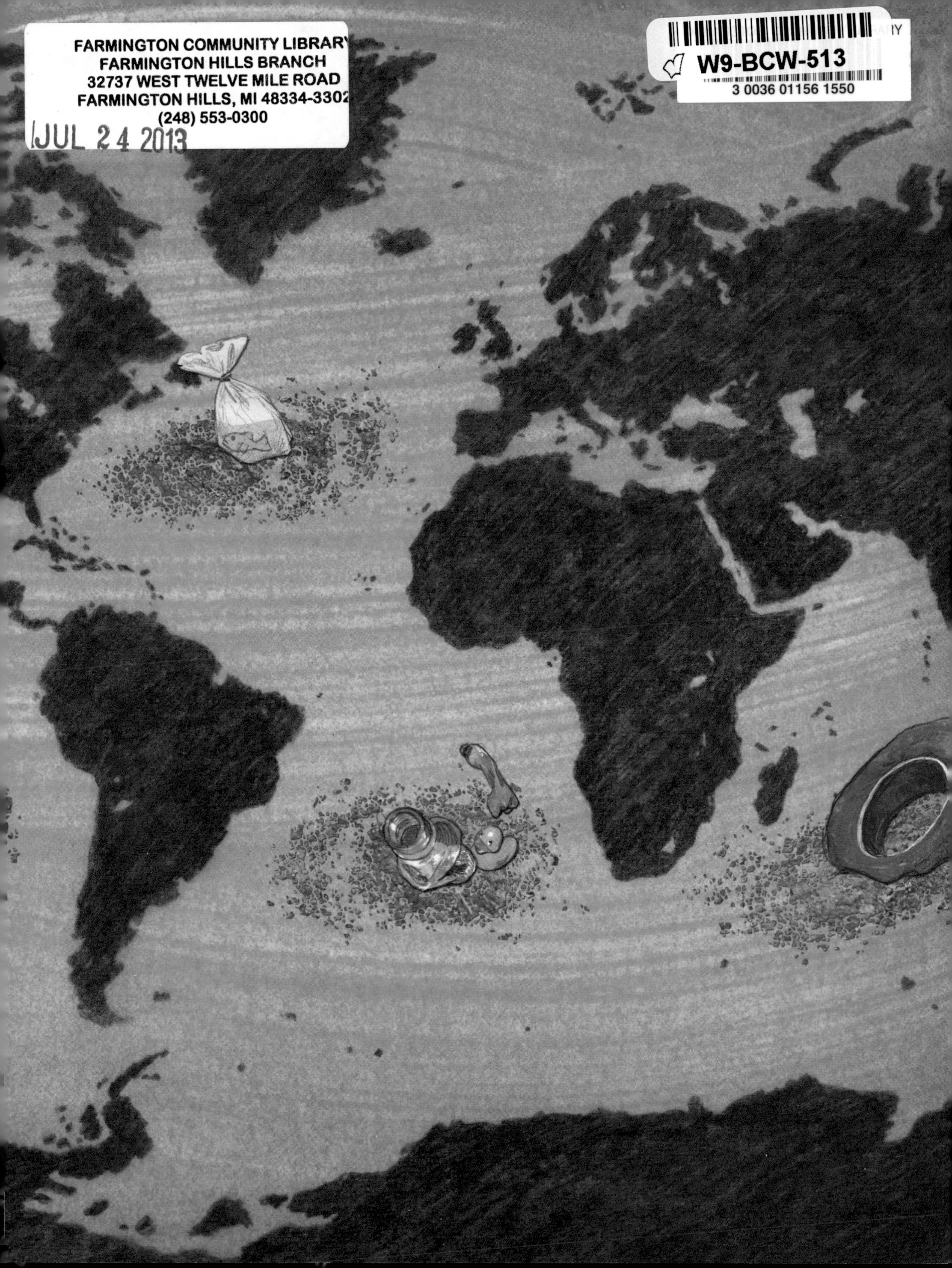

# I'm not a plastic bag™

## A Graphic Novel

by Rachel Hope Allison

ARCHAIA™
ENTERTAINMENT LLC

JEFF CORWIN
CONNECT™

# I'm not a plastic bag™

Story and art by
## Rachel Hope Allison

Forward by
## Jeff Corwin

**Anurag Agarwal**, Global Citizen/Co-Founder, JeffCorwinConnect™ Inc.
**Rebecca Taylor**, Editor
**Fawn Lau**, Design
**Scott Newman**, Production Manager

Archaia Entertainment LLC

**PJ Bickett**, CEO
**Mark Smylie**, CCO
**Mike Kennedy**, Publisher
**Stephen Christy**, Editor-in-Chief

Published by Archaia.

Archaia Entertainment LLC
1680 Vine Street, Suite 1010
Los Angeles, CA, 90028, USA
www.archaia.com

Archaia Entertainment & Global Printing, Sourcing & Development (Global PSD),
in association with American Forests® and the Global ReLeaf® programs, will plant
two trees for each tree used in the manufacturing of this book. Global ReLeaf® is an
international campaign by American Forests®, the nation's oldest nonprofit conservation
organization and a world leader in planting trees for environmental restoration.

I'M NOT A PLASTIC BAG. Original Graphic Novel Hardcover.
April 2012. FIRST PRINTING.

10 9 8 7 6 5 4 3 2 1

ISBN: 1-936393-54-9
ISBN-13: 978-1-936393-54-1

Printed in China by Global PSD.

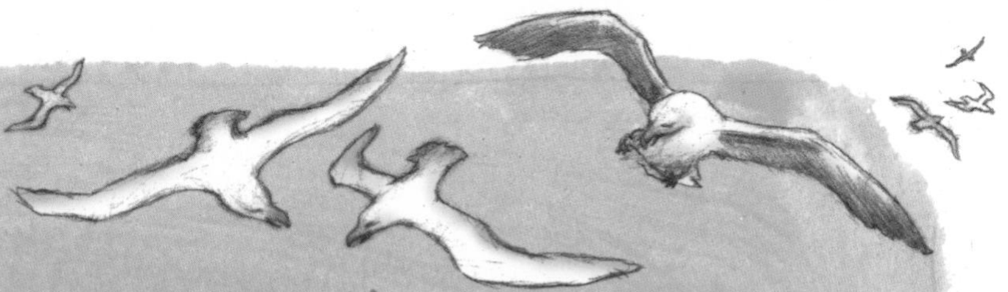

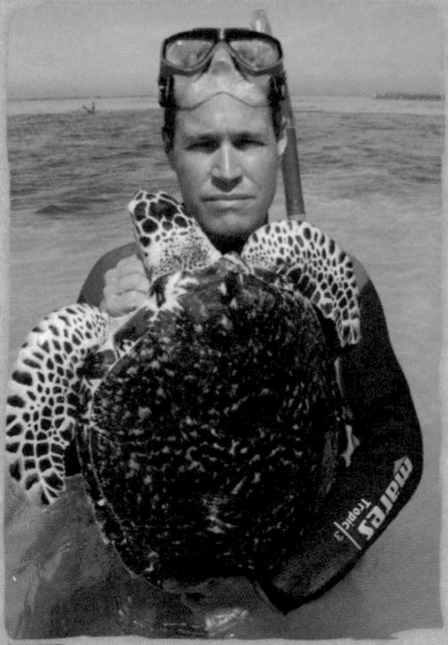

JEFFCORWINCONNECT™ INC.

# FOREWORD

Trash, waste, garbage, litter, refuse. These are just a few of the words we use to describe the unwanted material we produce and discard each day of our lives. While some of us may generate more rubbish than others, and while some folks might try a little harder to lessen it, precious few humans on Earth can avoid producing it. We fail to escape it, even as we attempt to discard, hide, sink, float, bury, and dump it.

So, just how much trash do we produce? Despite the fact that US citizens take up only 5% of the world population, we generate 40% of our planet's trash! Your average American produces nearly 5 pounds of non-biodegradable material each day, which nationally adds up to about 200 million tons of long-lived garbage. Globally, humankind burdens our planet with about 5 billion tons of trash every year. Out of all this trash, only 3% of it is recycled. What is even more staggering, most of the remaining refuse may last on our planet for as long as 400 years before it begins to break down.

The journey of discarded waste is wide-ranging and far-reaching. A flyaway sheet of plastic tarp may end up smothering a living boulder of coral reef, while a produce bag from a distant supermarket, masquerading as a jellyfish, could find its way into the belly of an endangered sea turtle. The sad and simple truth is that our monstrous output of trash has made our planet a very dirty and dangerous place. The good news is that each one of us, no matter where you are from, or how old you are, has the power and the responsibility to keep our Earth clean.

I truly believe that when it comes to conserving our planet's natural resources, wildlife, and ecology, we rarely protect what we fail to appreciate, and we only appreciate what we understand. If you are looking for a powerful story to inspire responsible environmental stewardship, you will find it in the pages of Rachel Hope Allison's *I'm Not a Plastic Bag*. Beautifully and poignantly illustrated, this book transforms the convoluted process of global waste into a magical and spellbinding journey.

Rachel Allison's incredible and almost ethereal story of the Great Pacific Garbage Patch will not only engage and awaken your spirit, but will empower all of us to save our precious planet from falling prey to garbage and waste. This tale forcefully reminds us that the world we inhabit today is not inherited from our ancestors, but borrowed from our children.

Jeff Corwin

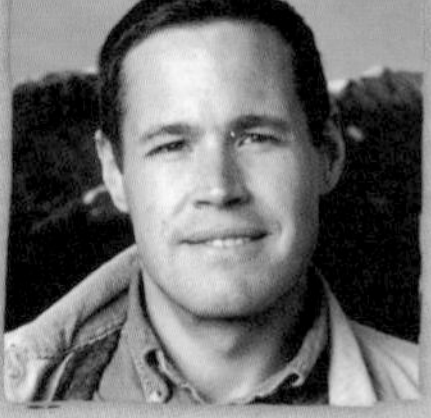

JEFFCORWINCONNECT™ INC.

## About Jeff

*Emmy-winning television host, author and biologist Jeff Corwin has worked for the conservation of endangered species, natural resources, and ecosystems around the globe. Jeff is executive producer and host of* Ocean Mysteries *on ABC. In addition to exploring the state of our planet's oceans and marine life, Jeff is a correspondent for MSNBC and NBC news. Beyond television, Jeff is an author, film producer, philanthropist, and educator. He is a co-founder of JeffCorwinConnect Inc.*

For Penny, Rick,
Robin, and Molly,
the most amazing second
family a girl could hope for.

Many, many thanks to everyone who helped me find my
way to—and stick with—this book. All my love and thanks to
Frances Jetter, Carl Smith, Jessica Gonzales, Mari Webel,
Josh Kobrin, Gaurav Misra, Madeline Neighly, Leslie Nguyen,
Bob Stein, my family, and pretty much everyone involved
in the SVA Illustration as Visual Essay program.

Special thanks also to Nate Folkert, Michelle Neuringer, and
John Smylie—without that serendipitous wedding conversation,
this book wouldn't have found a home at Archaia. And finally,
many thanks to Mark Smylie at Archaia, my amazing editor
Rebecca Taylor, Nicholas Mallos and Sonya Besteiro from the
Ocean Conservancy, and the JeffCorwinConnect™ team. I could
not have asked for smarter or more thoughtful partners in
bringing *I'm not a plastic bag* to life. You guys are the best!

# one

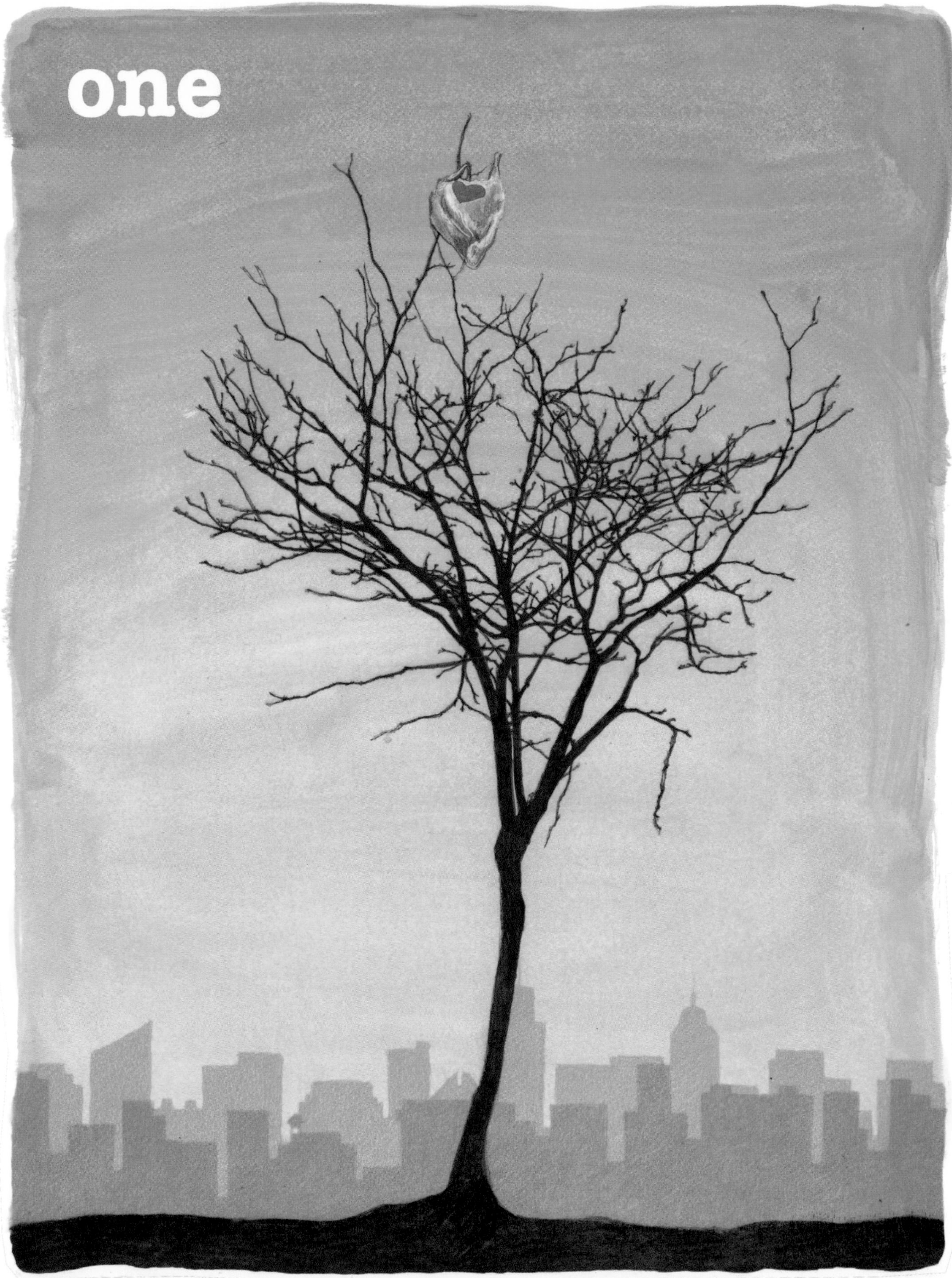

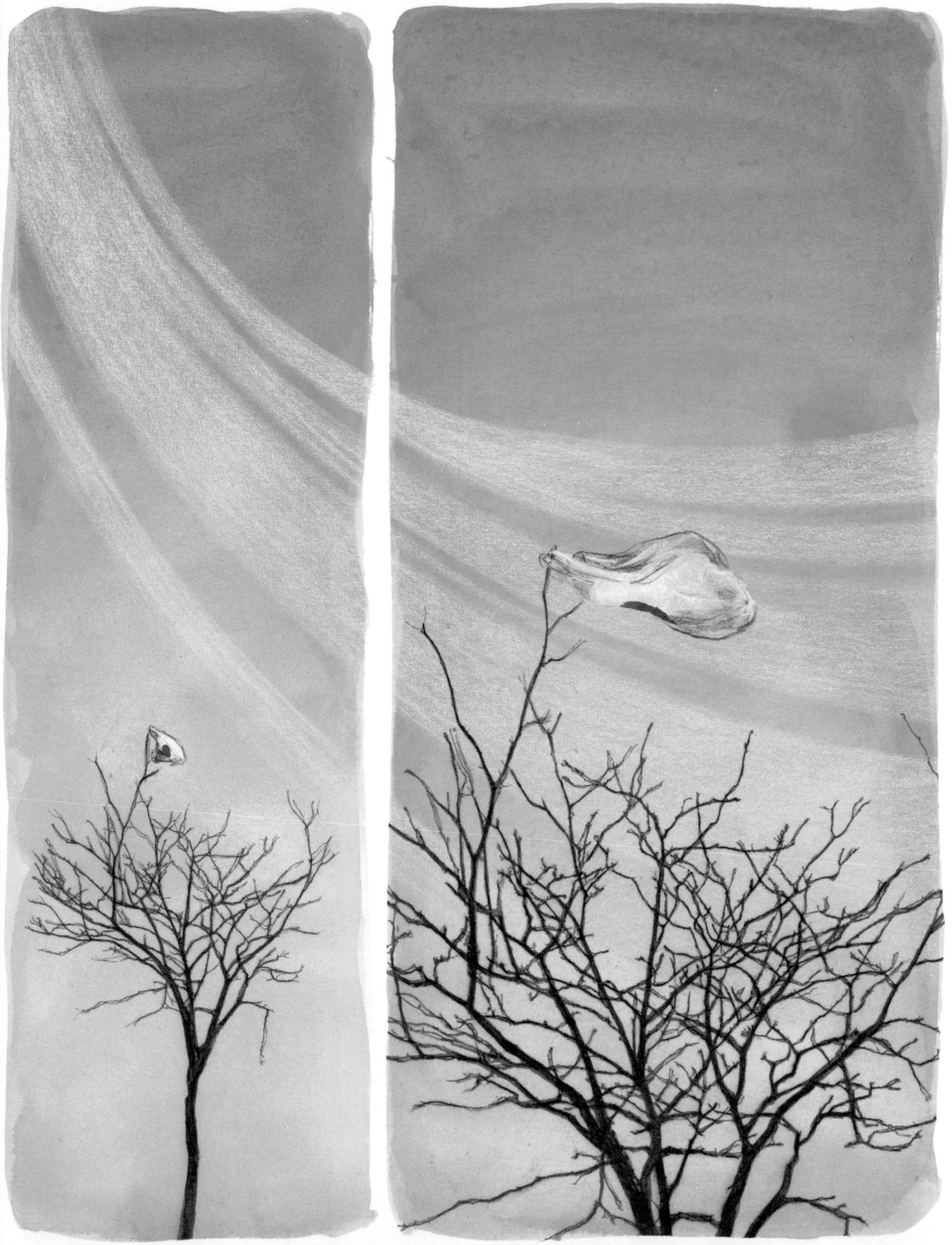

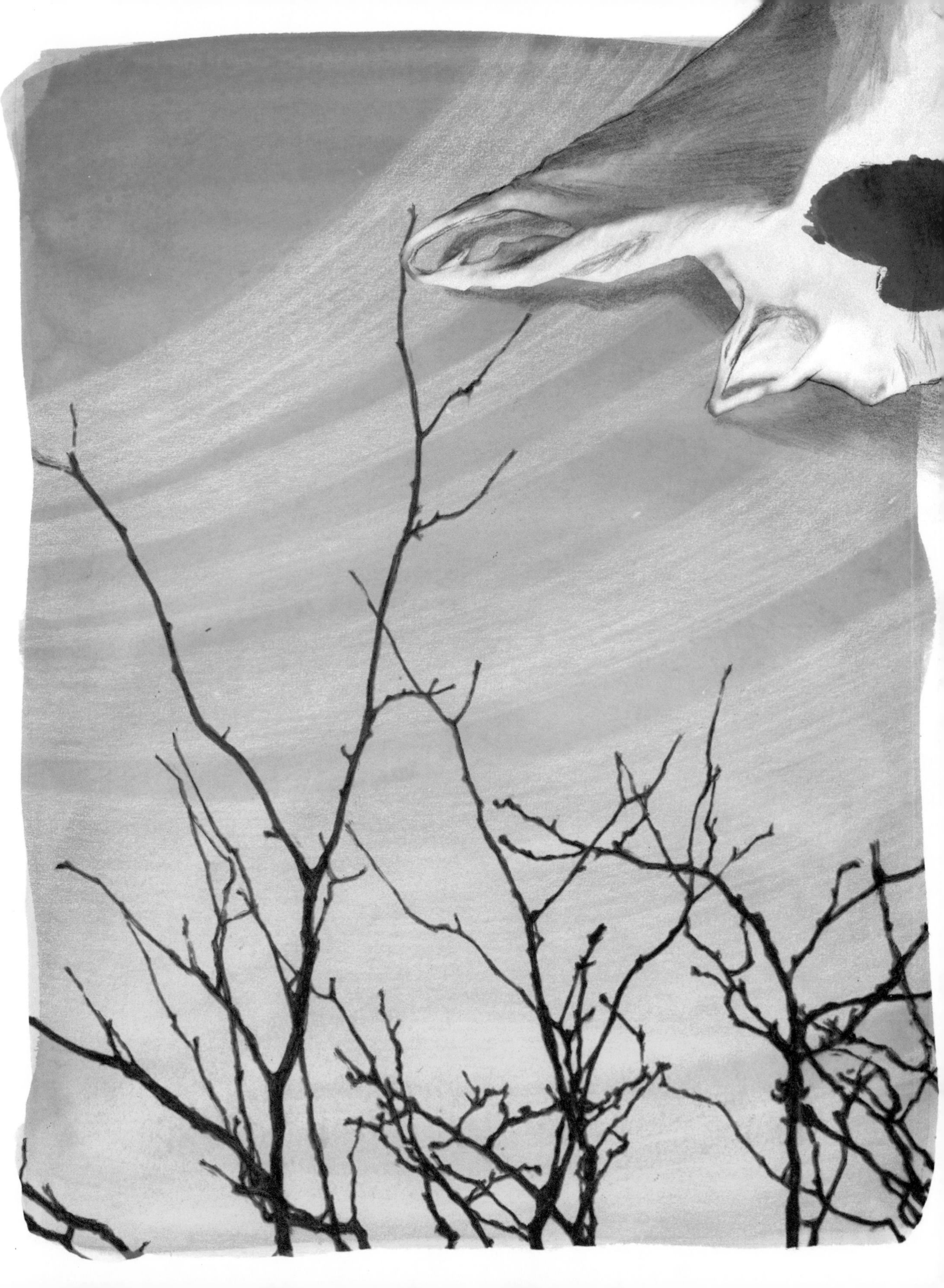

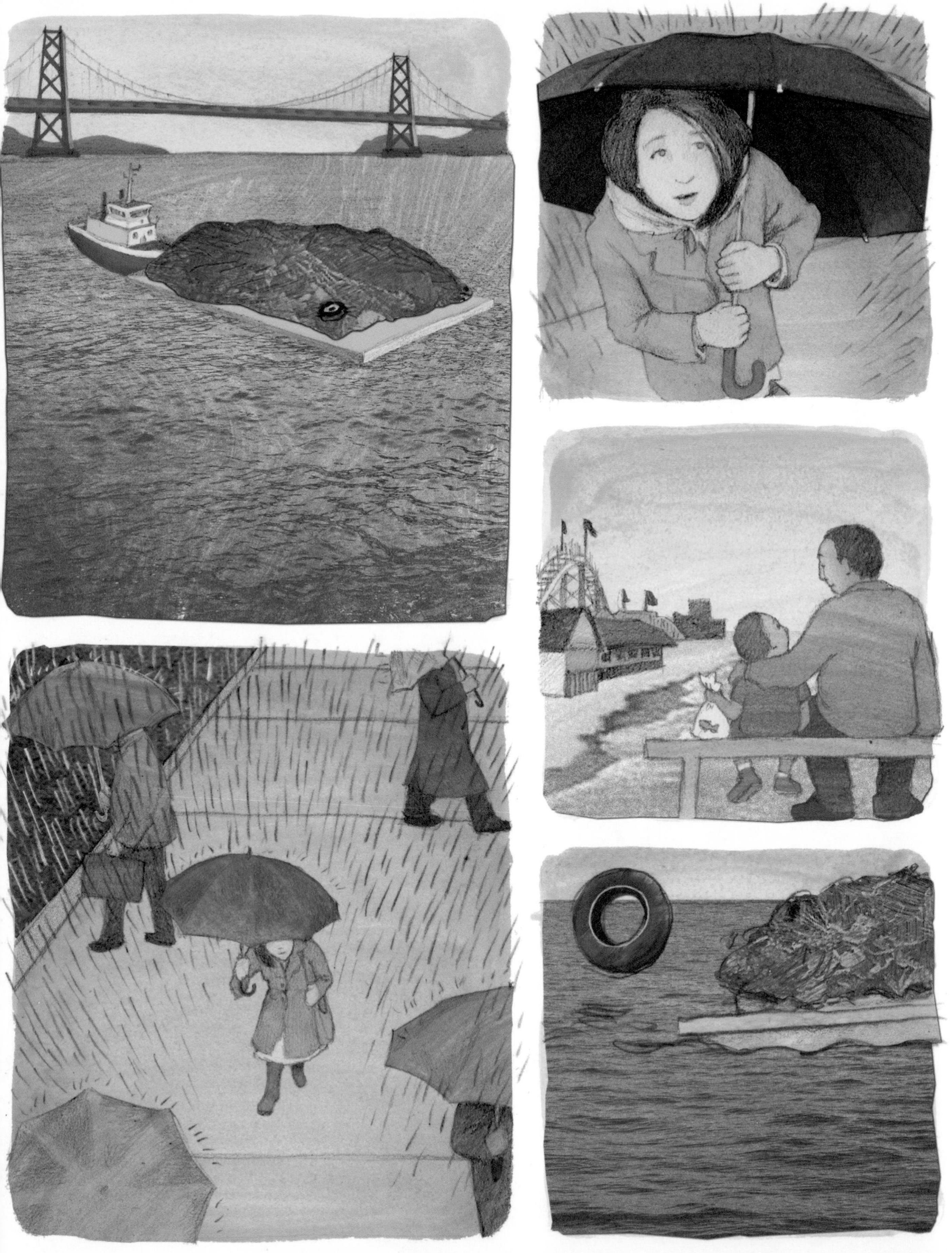

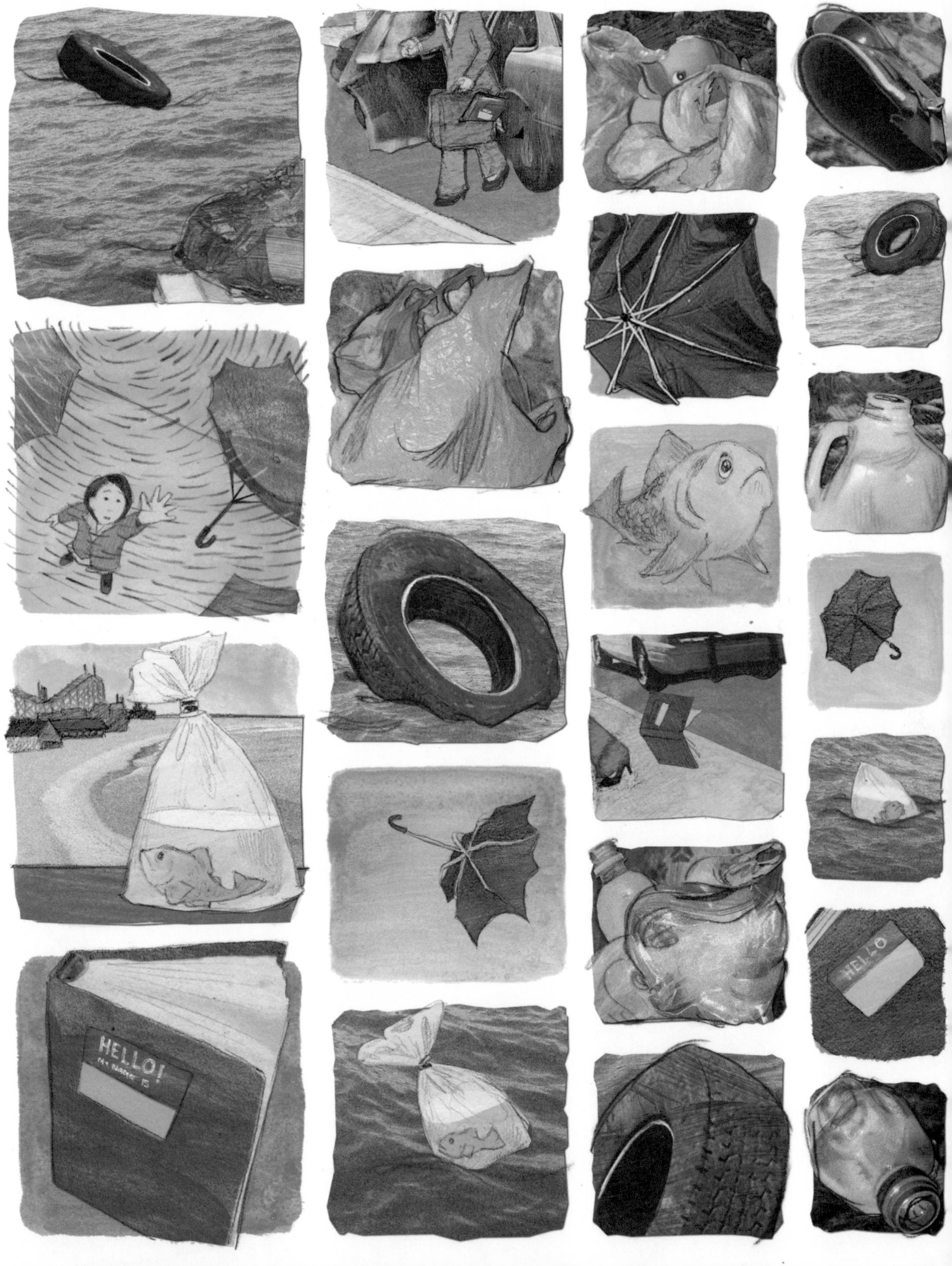
HELLO!
MY NAME IS
HELLO

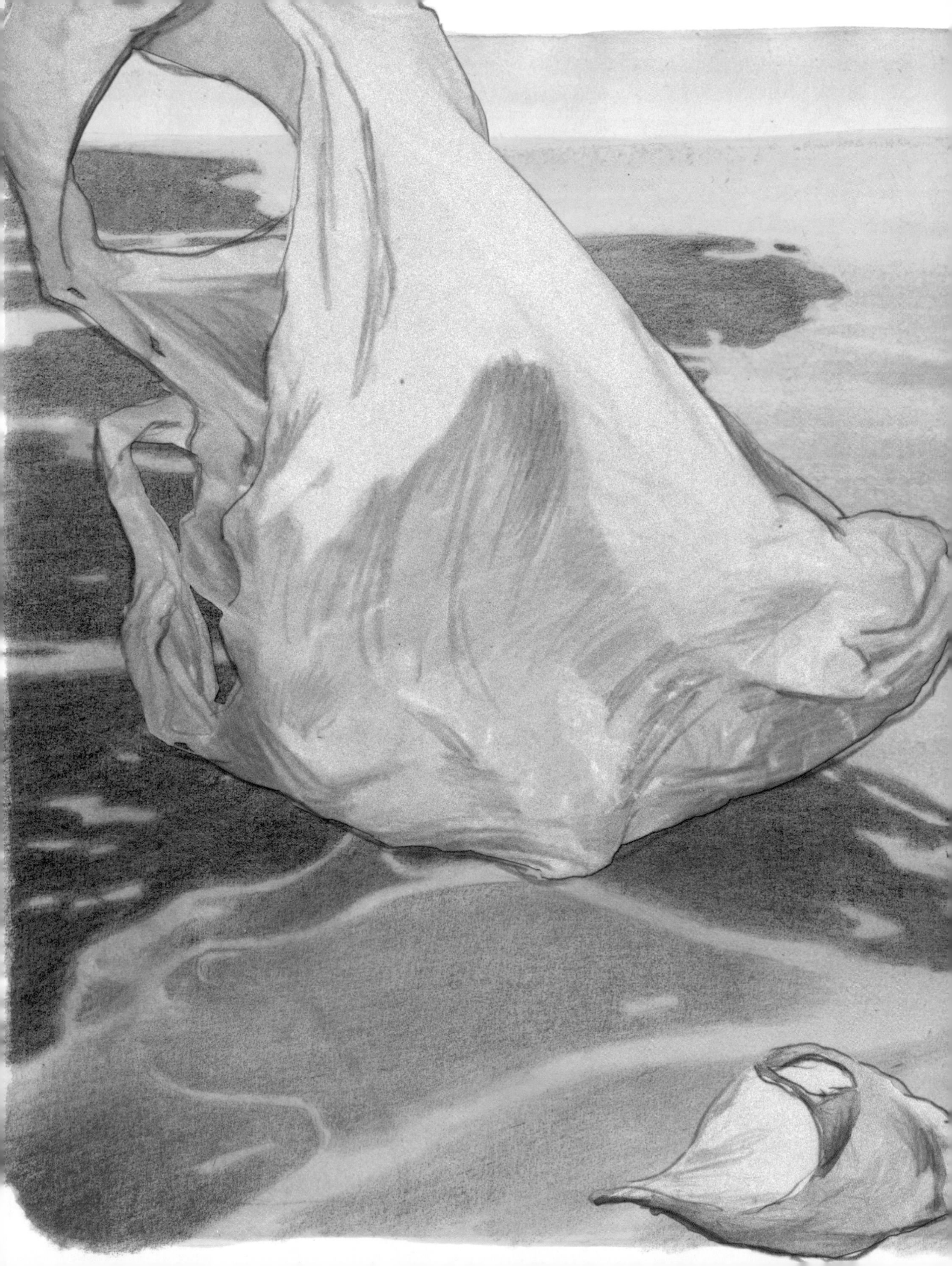

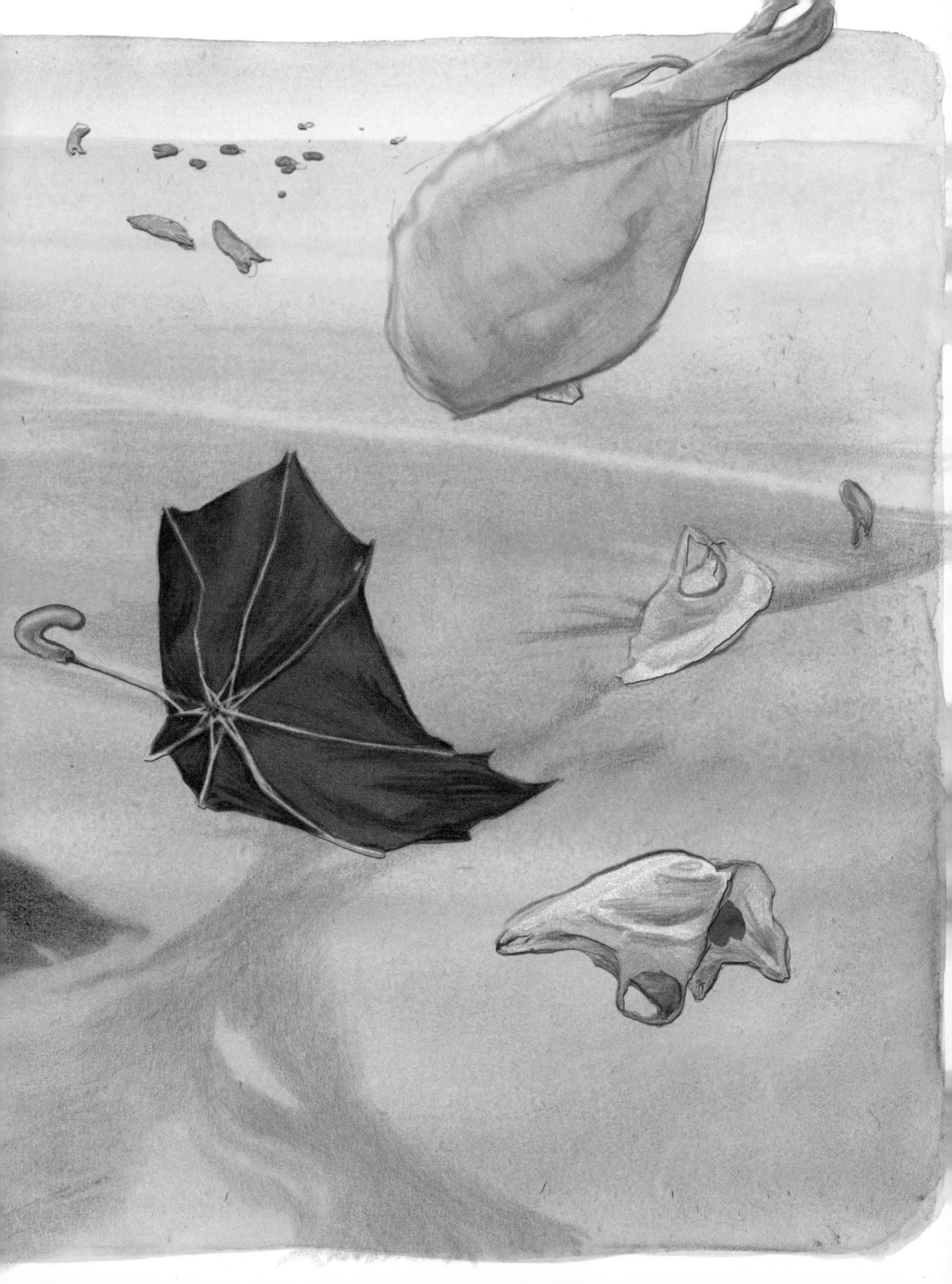

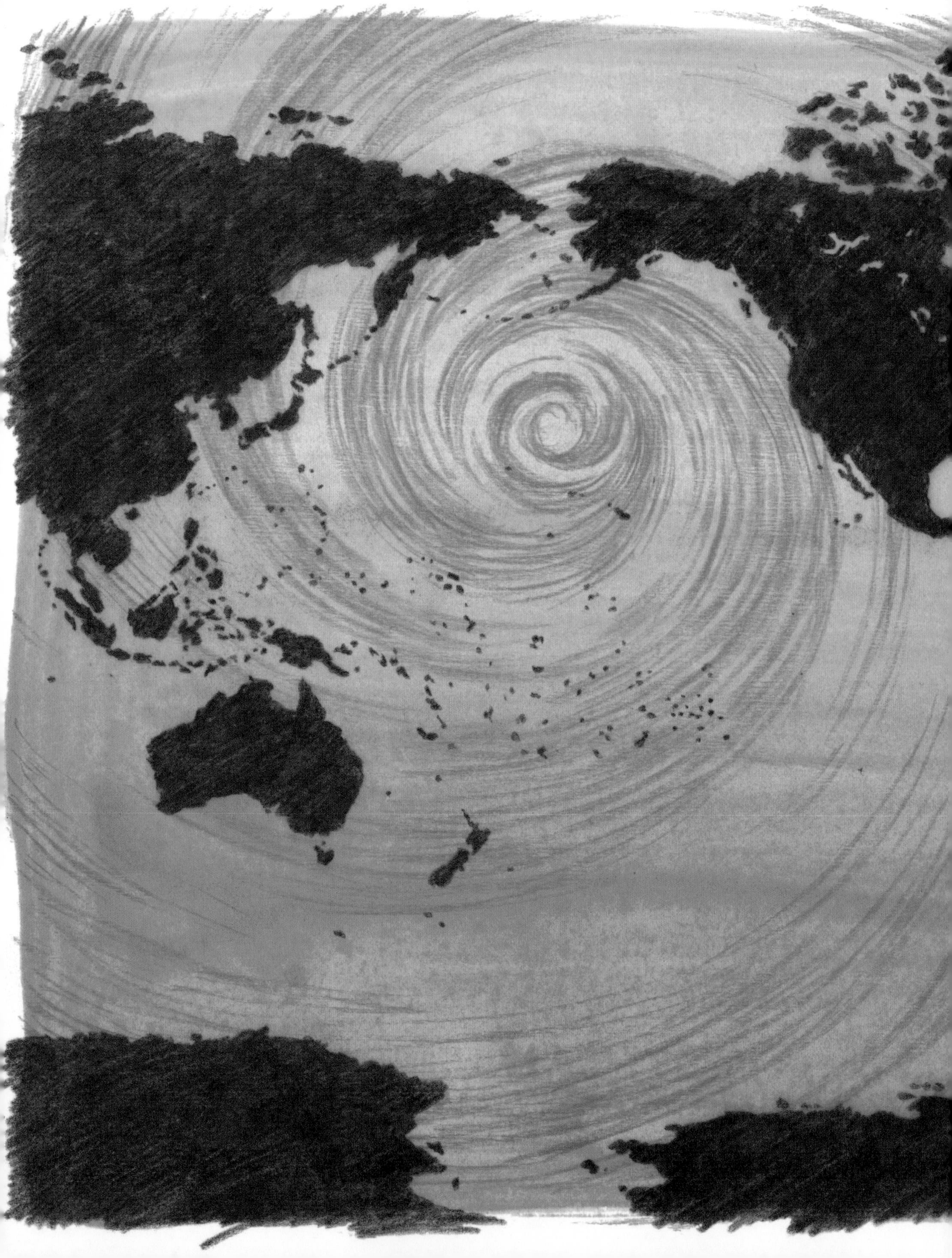

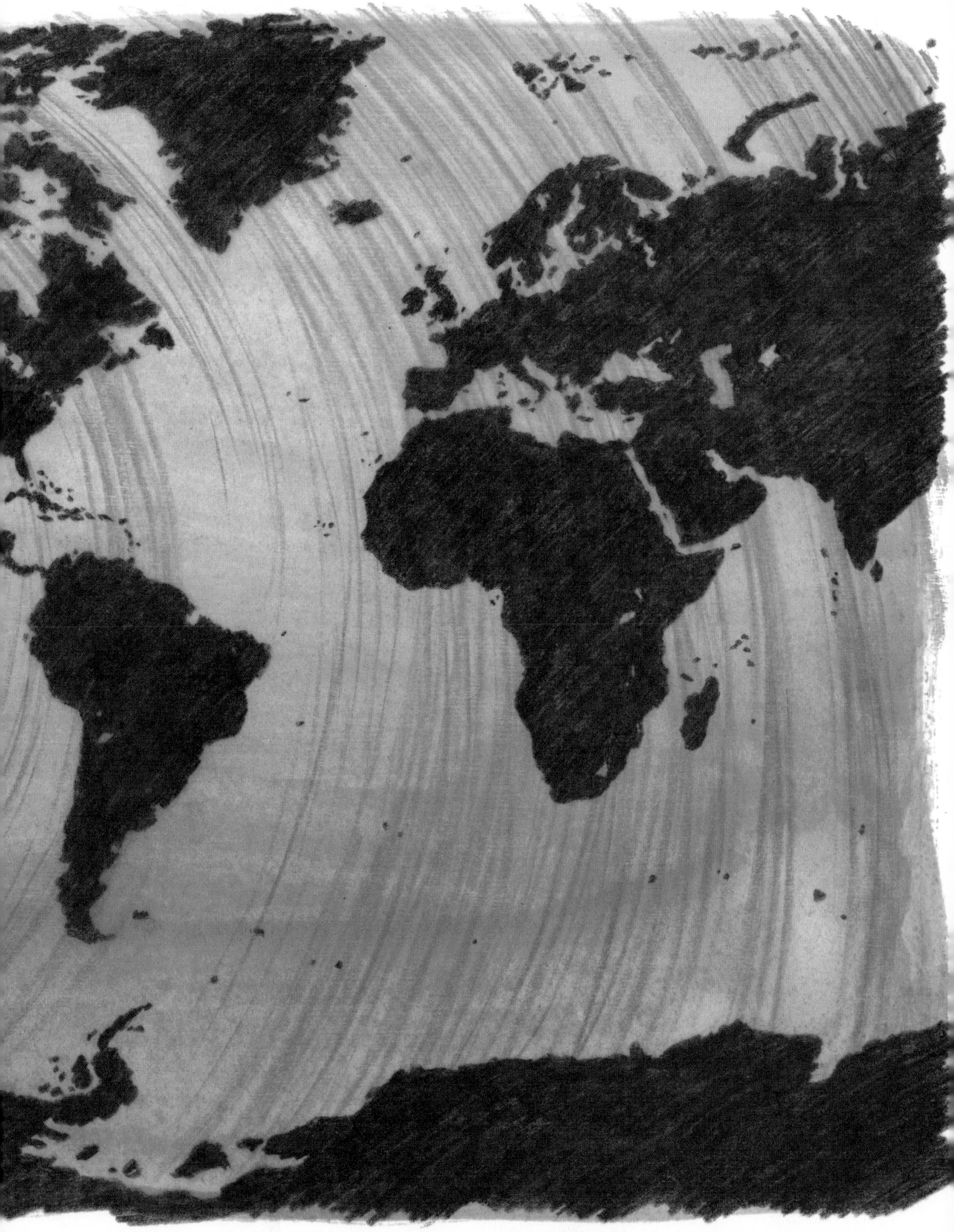

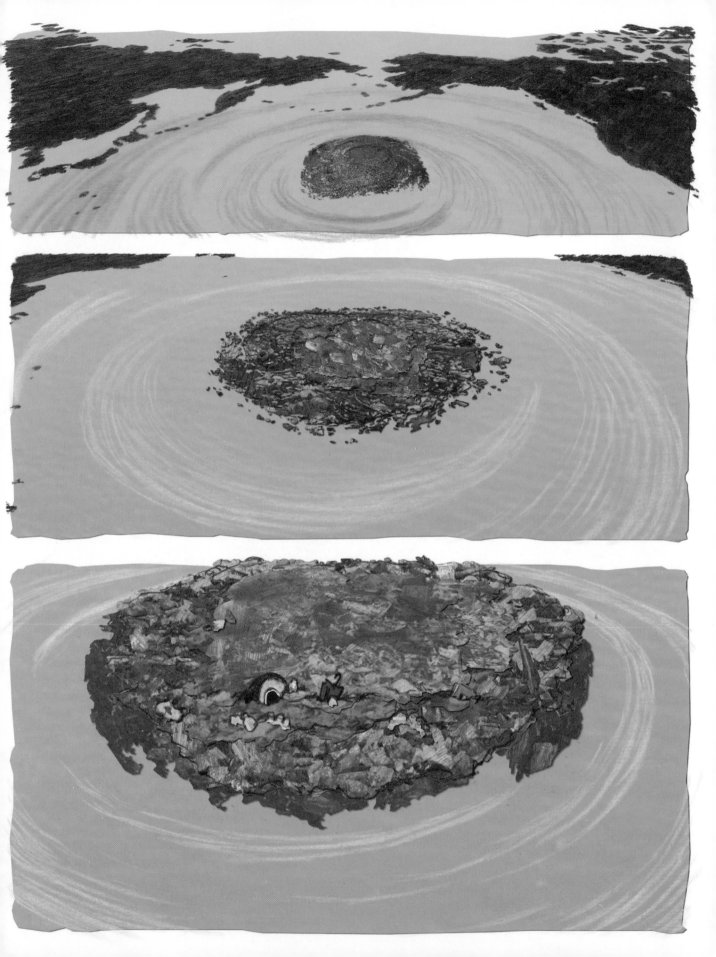

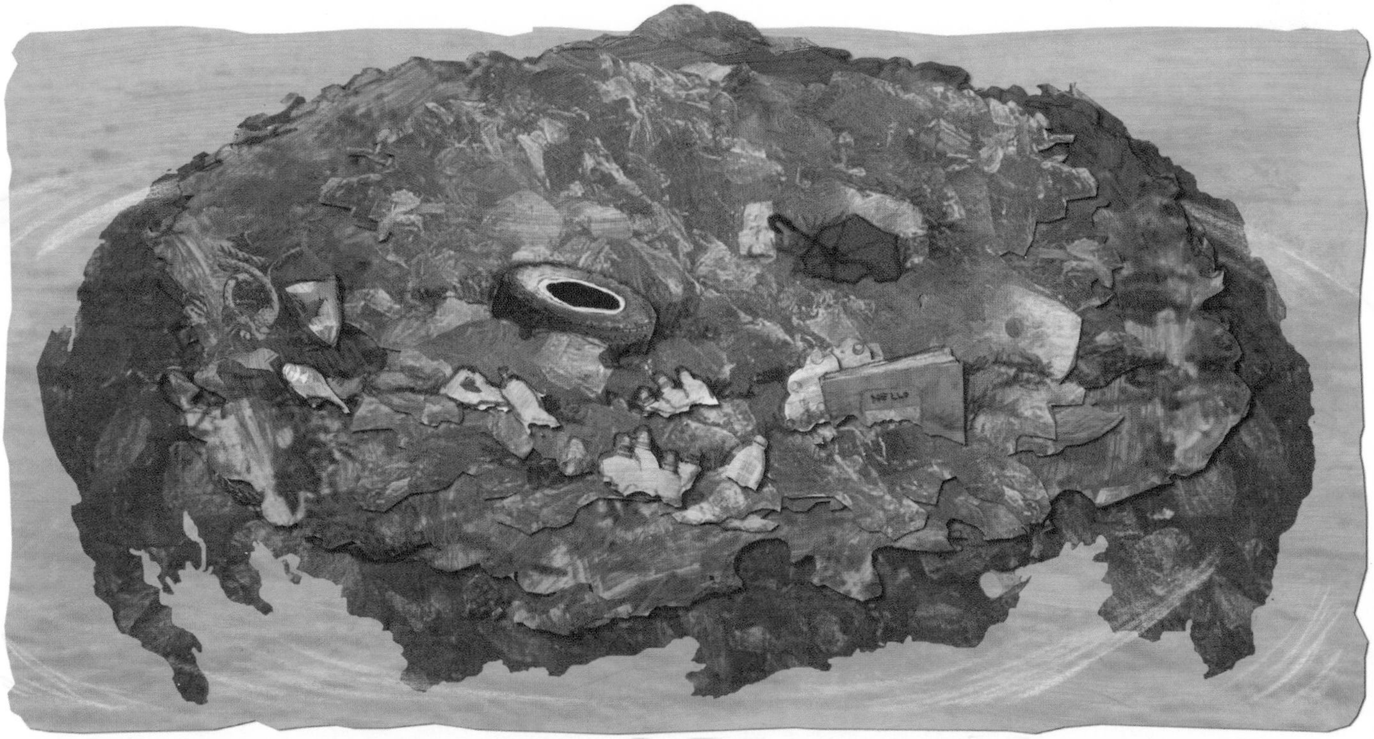

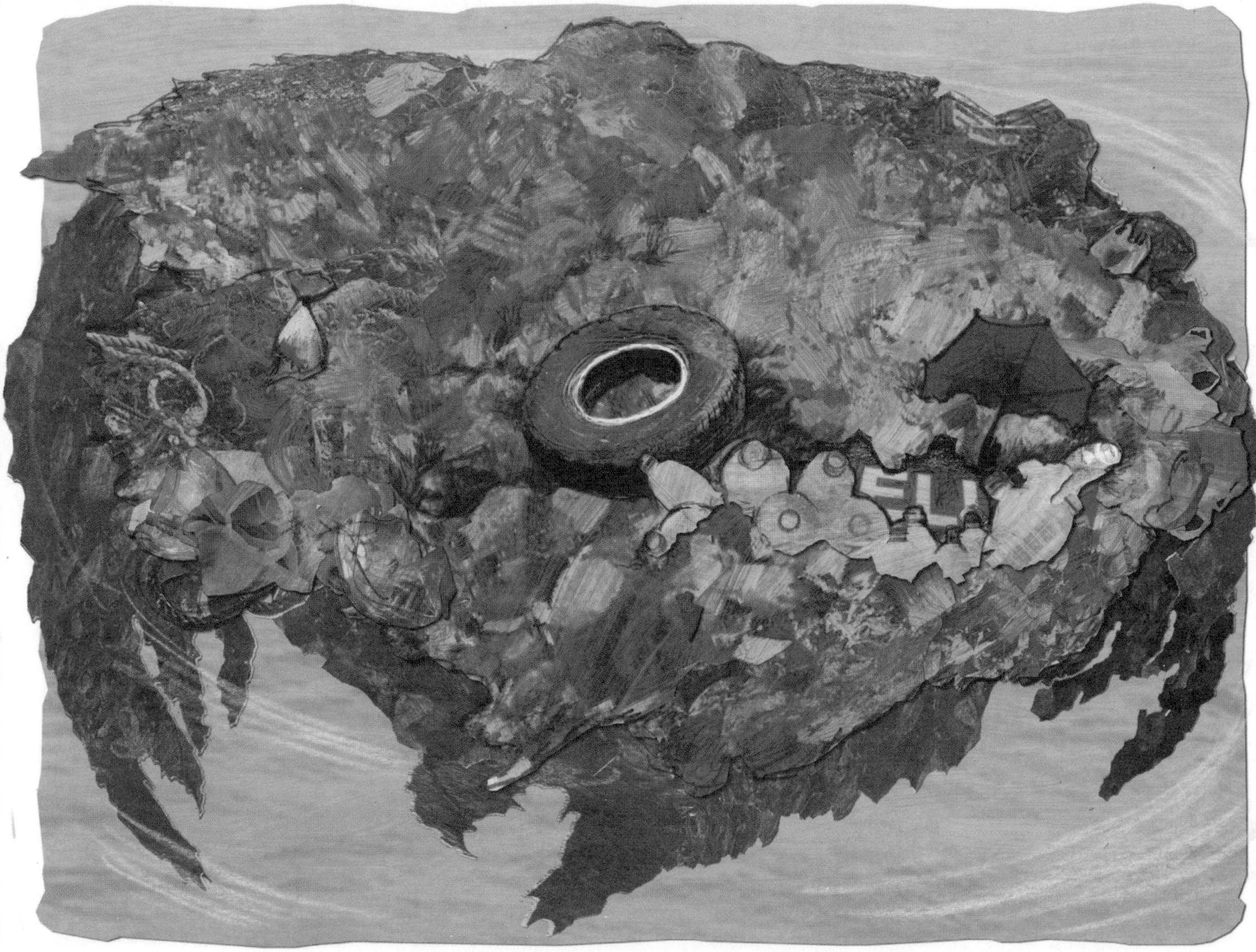

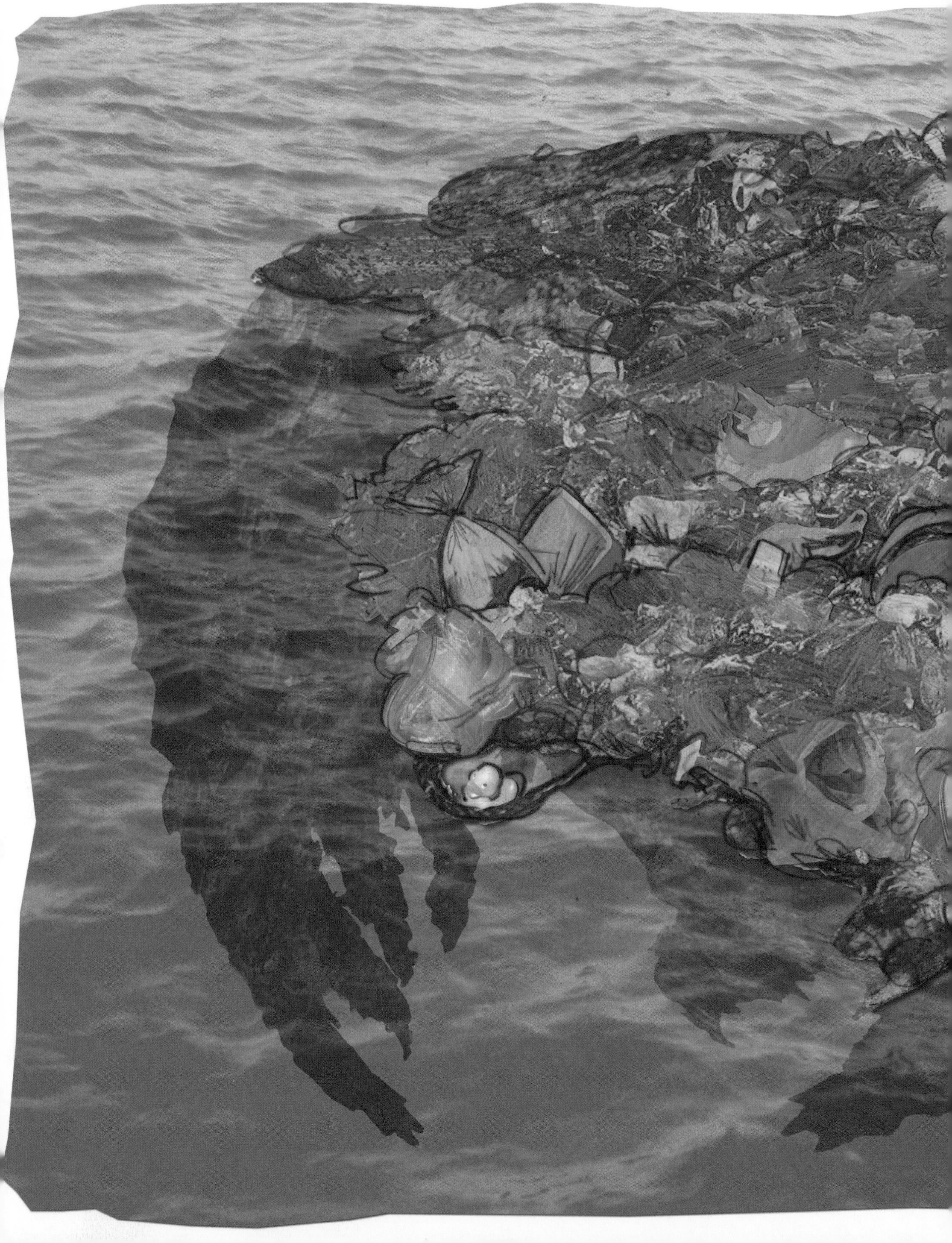

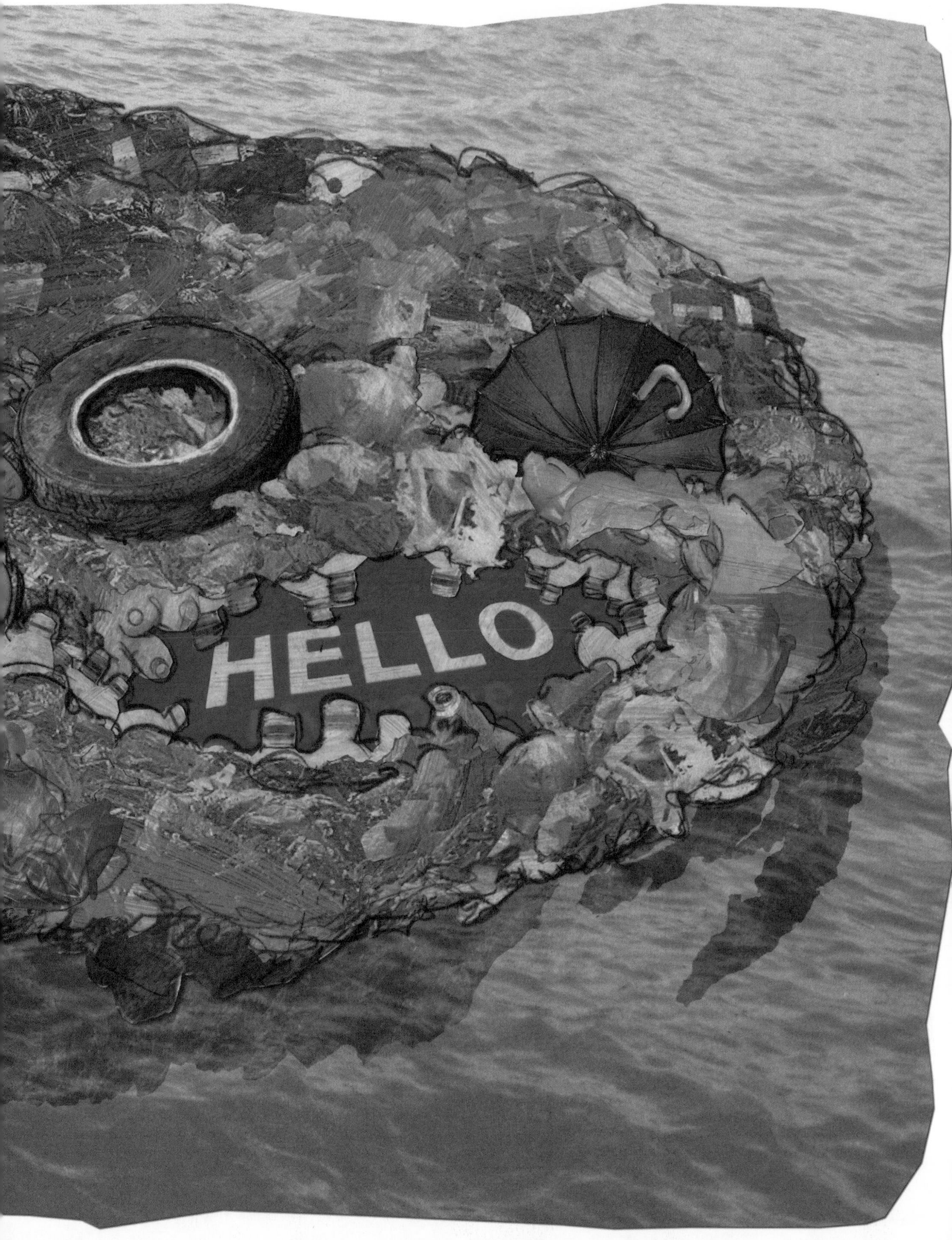
HELLO

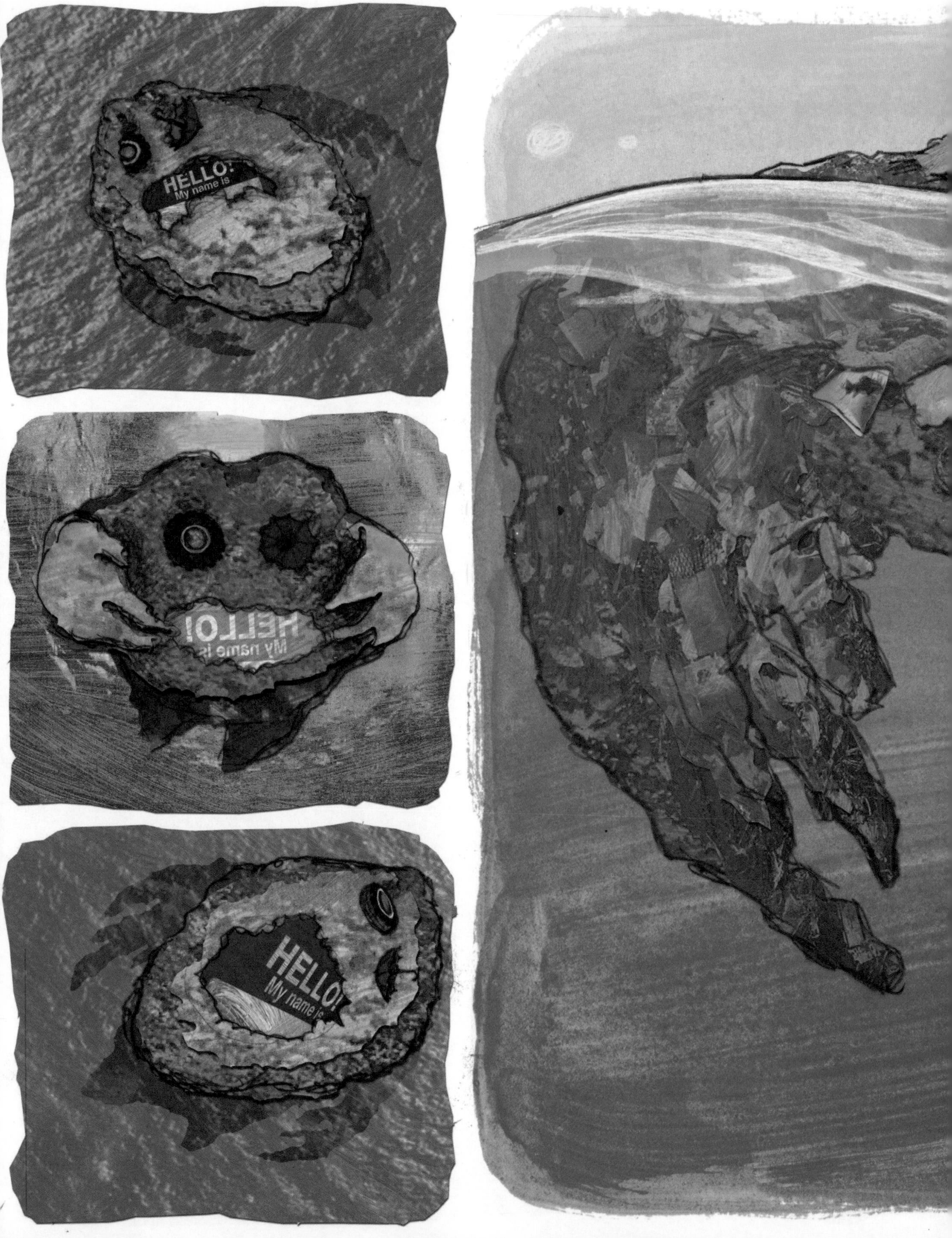
HELLO!
My name is
HELLO!
My name is
HELLO!
My name is

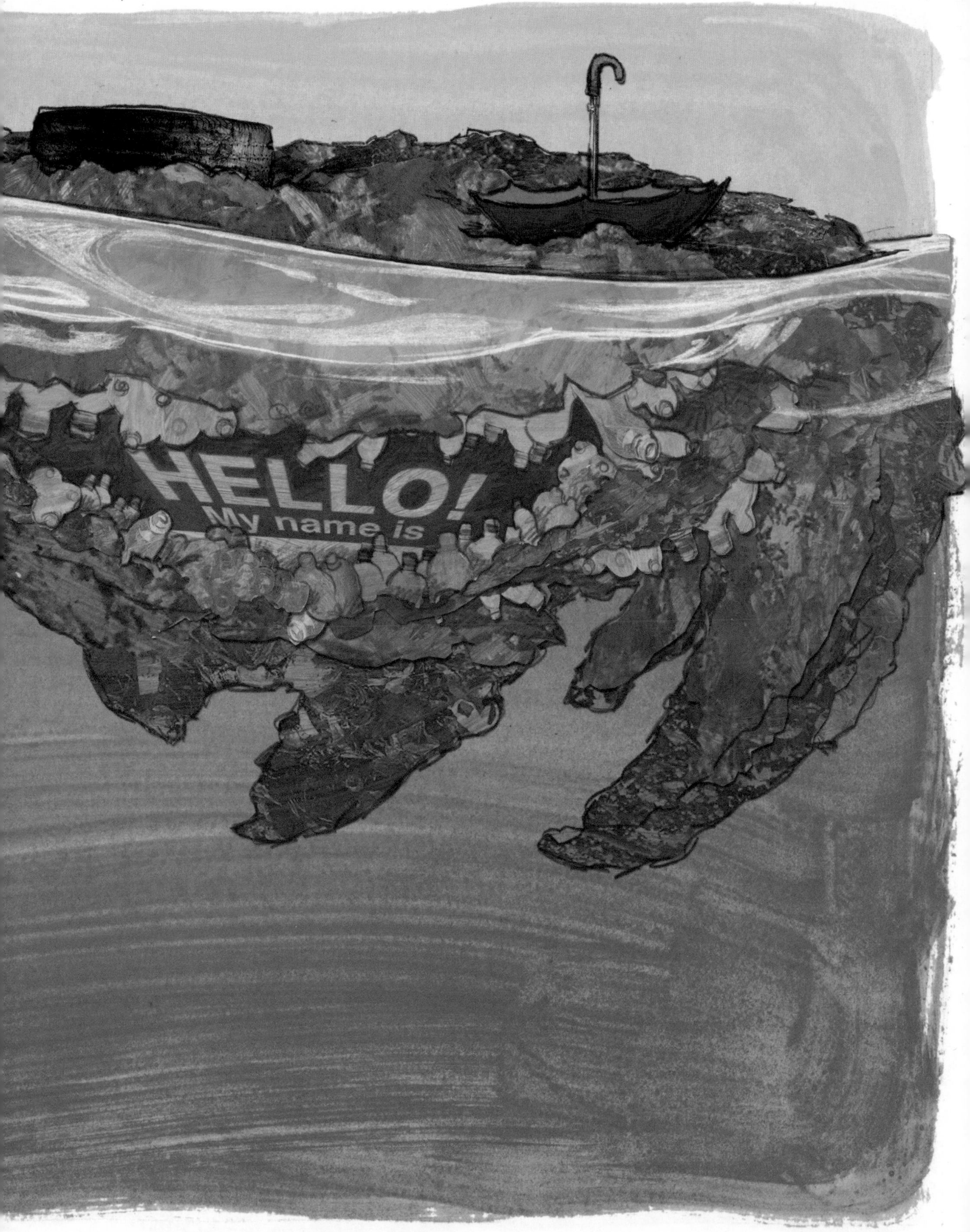
HELLO!
My name is

# two

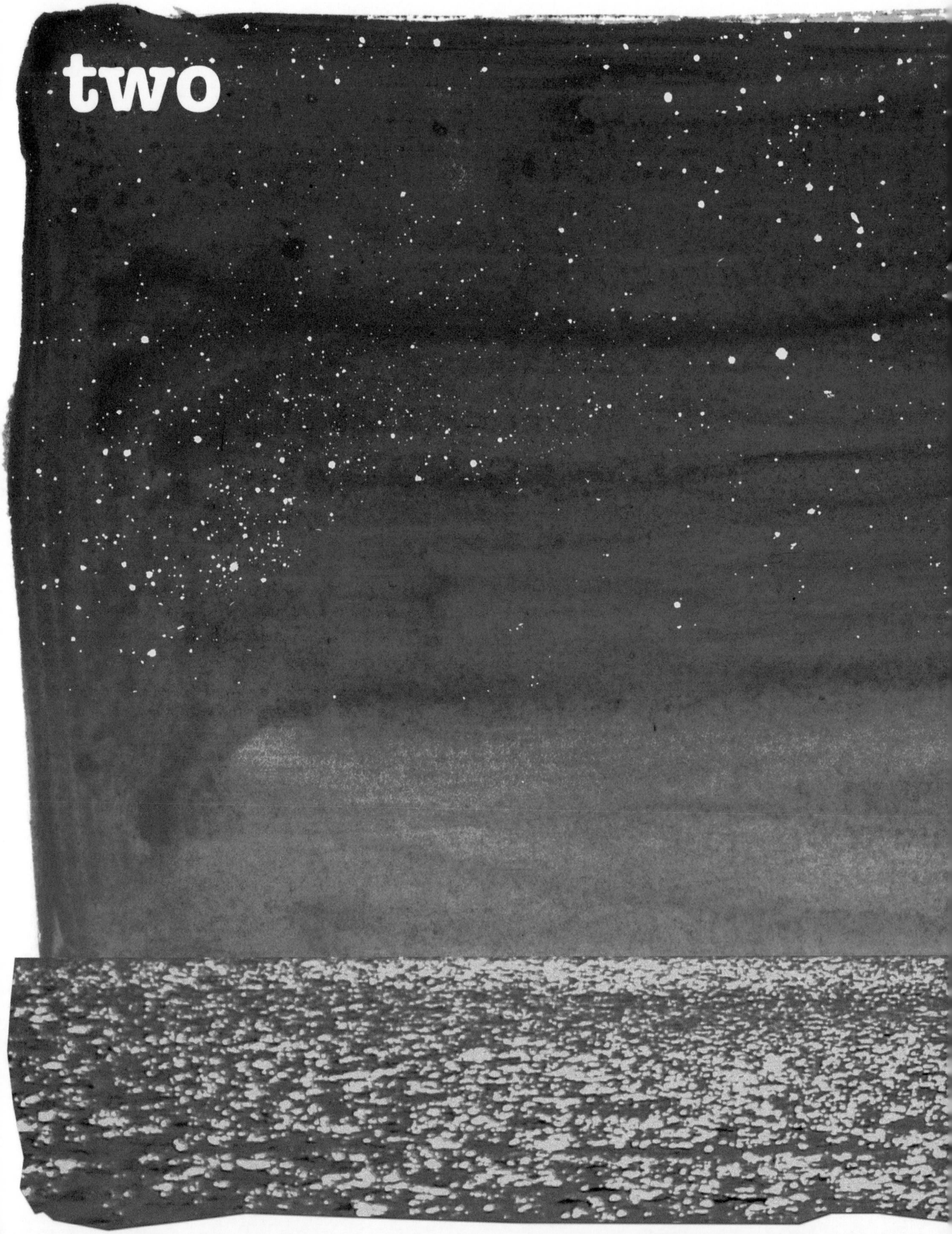

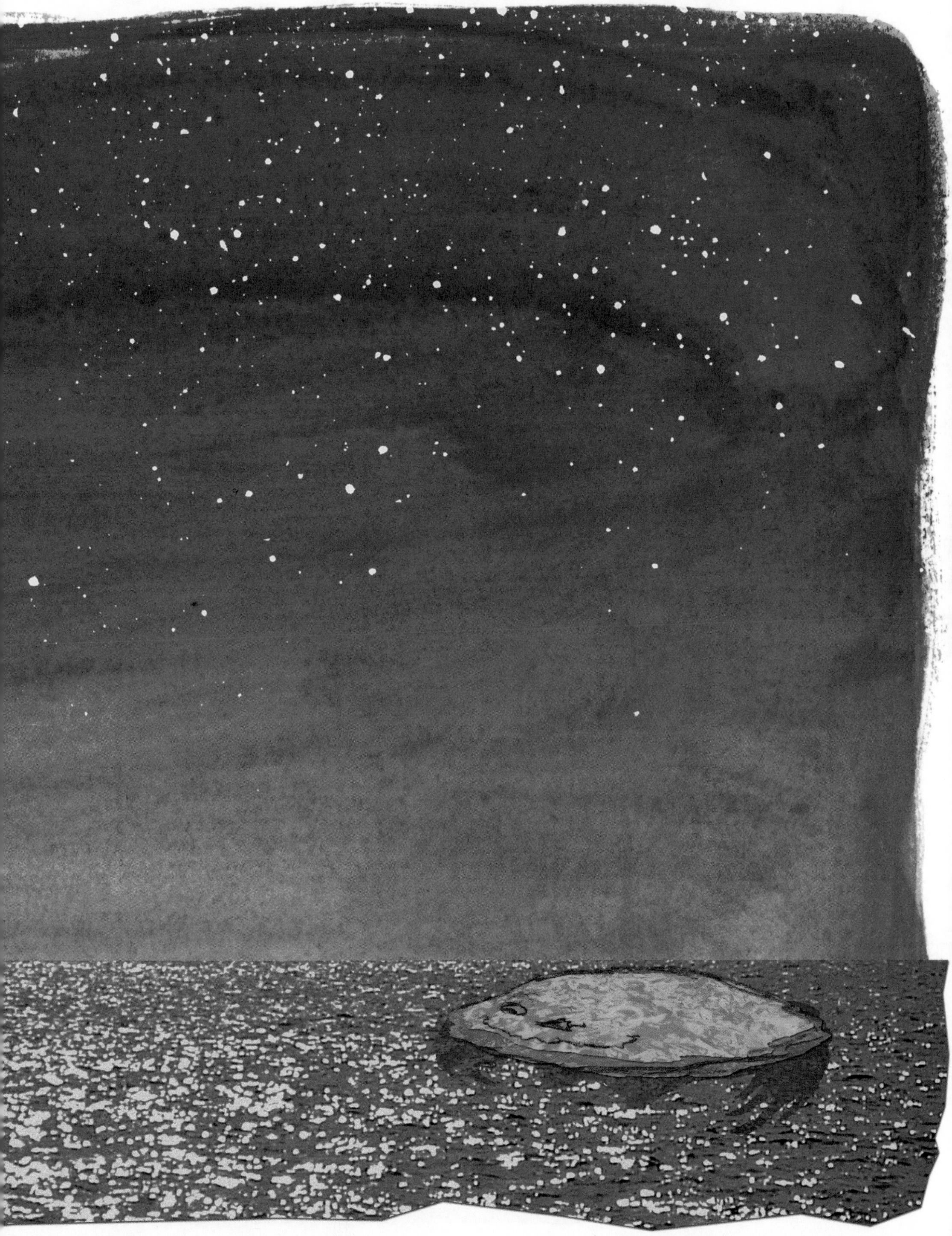

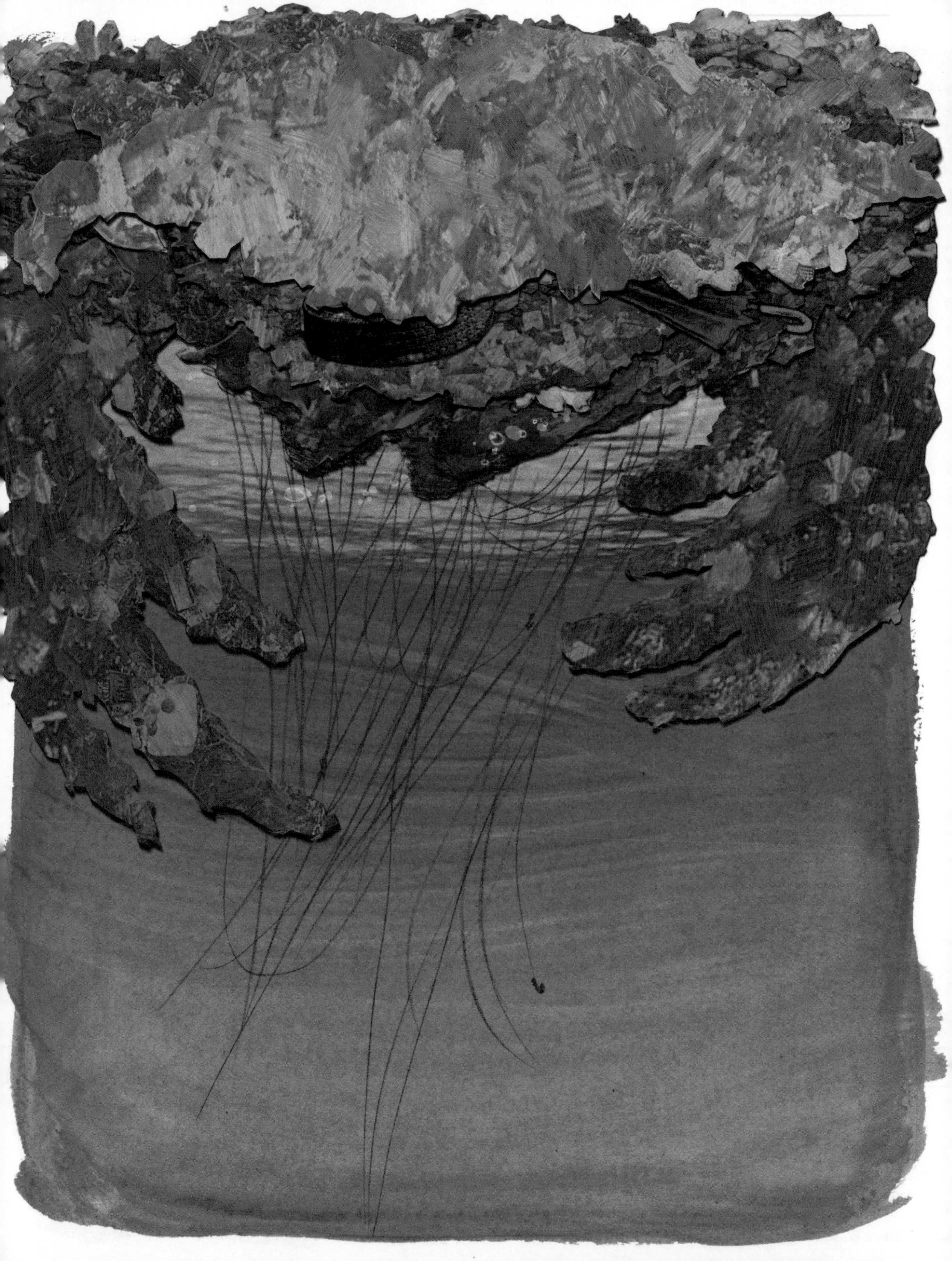

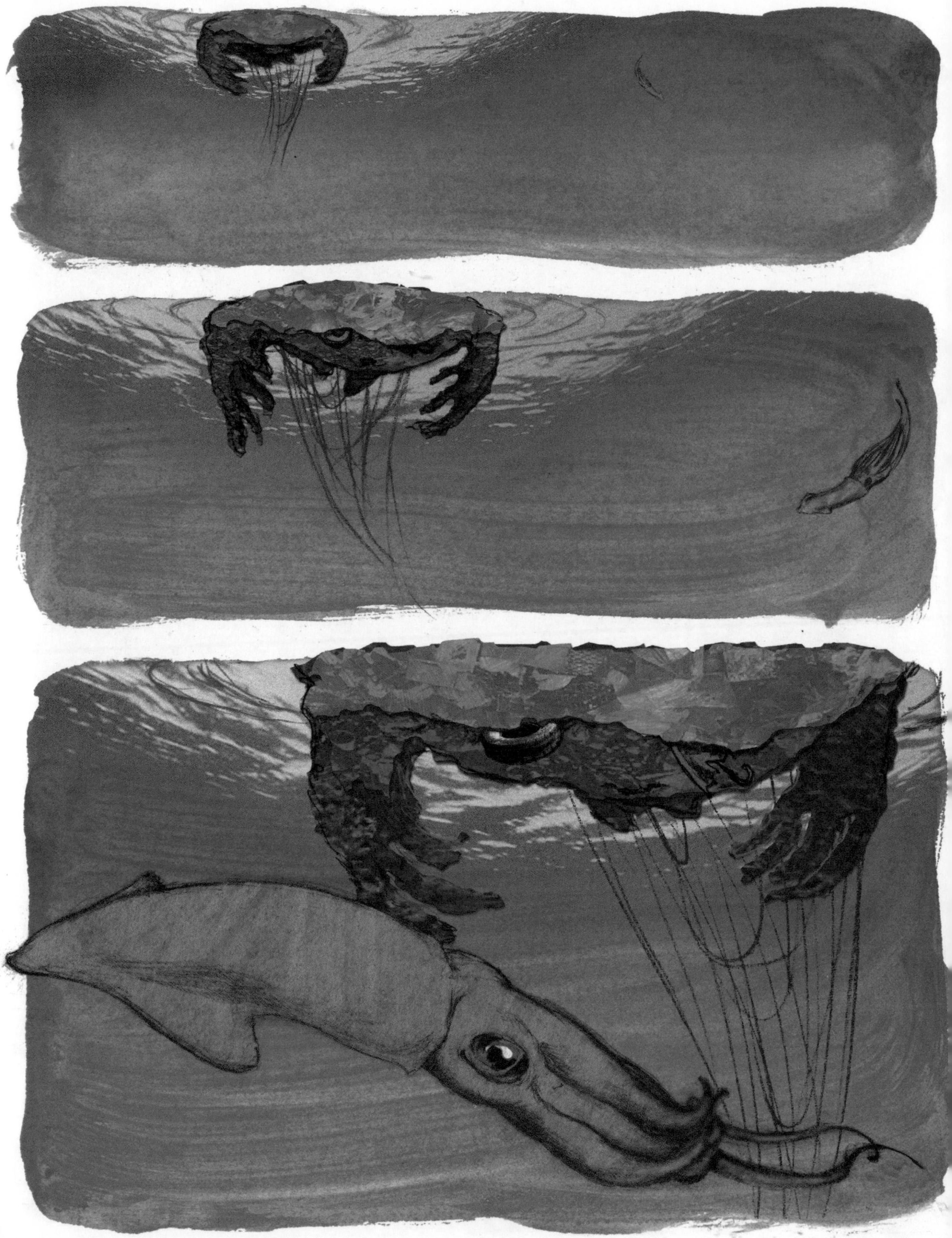

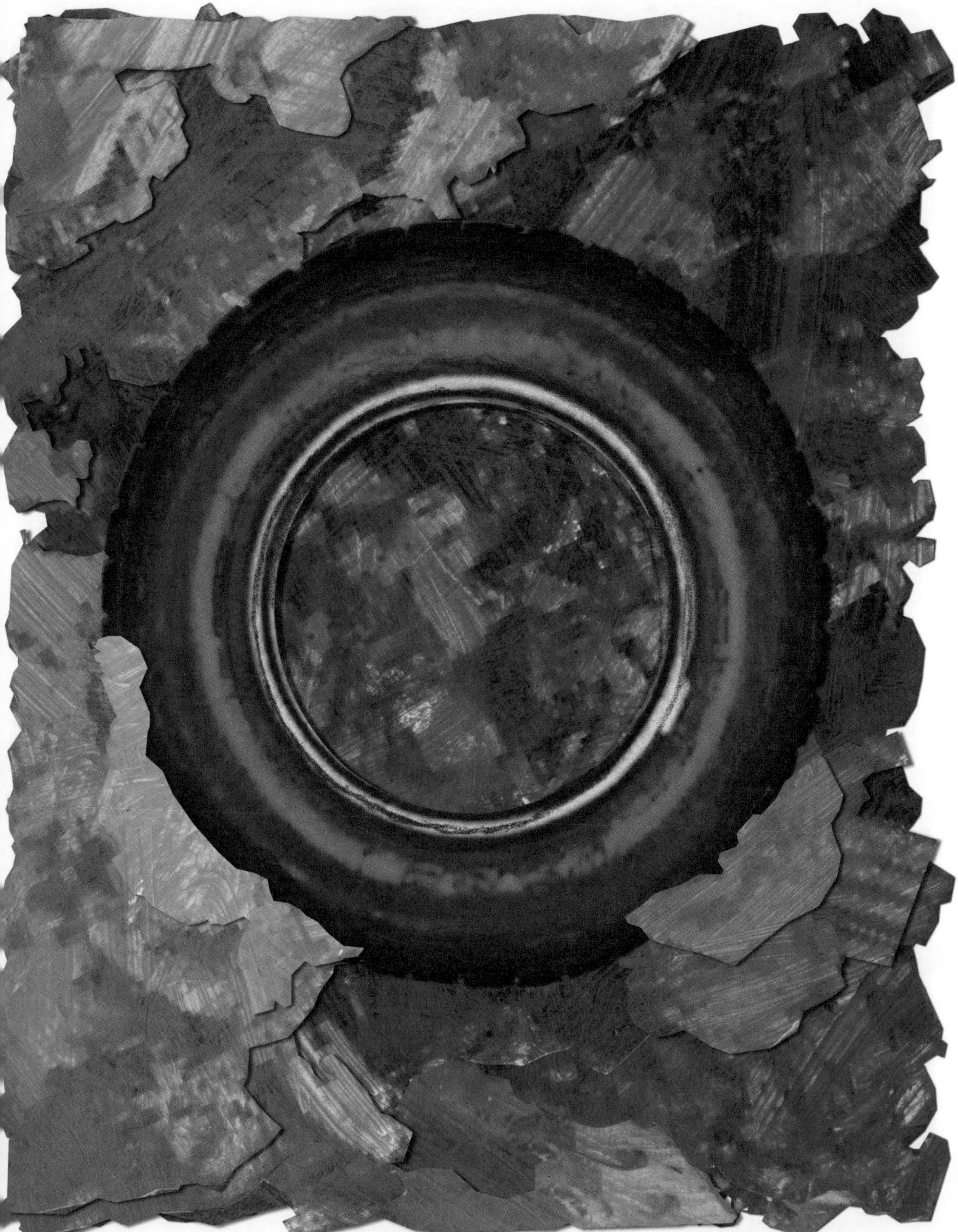

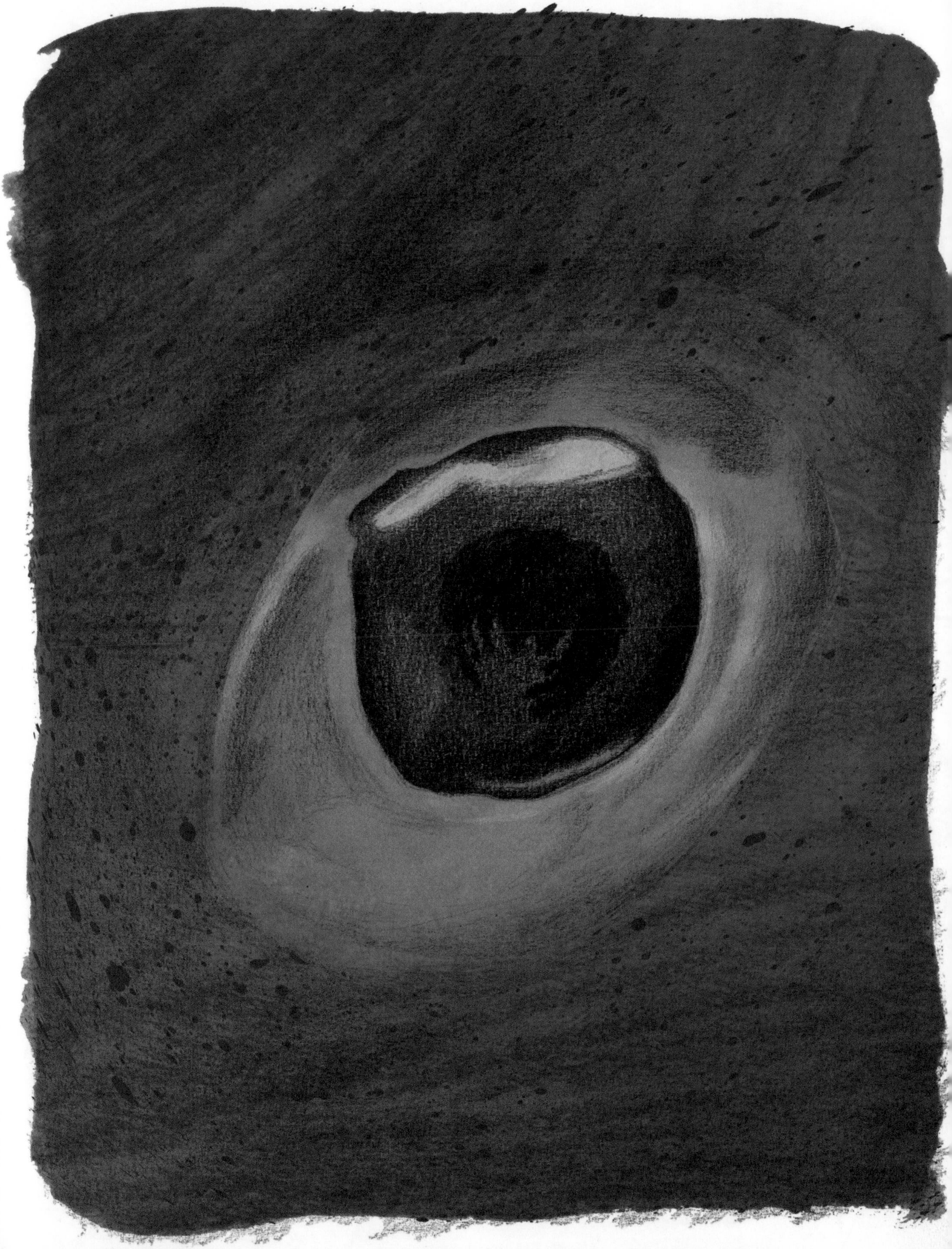

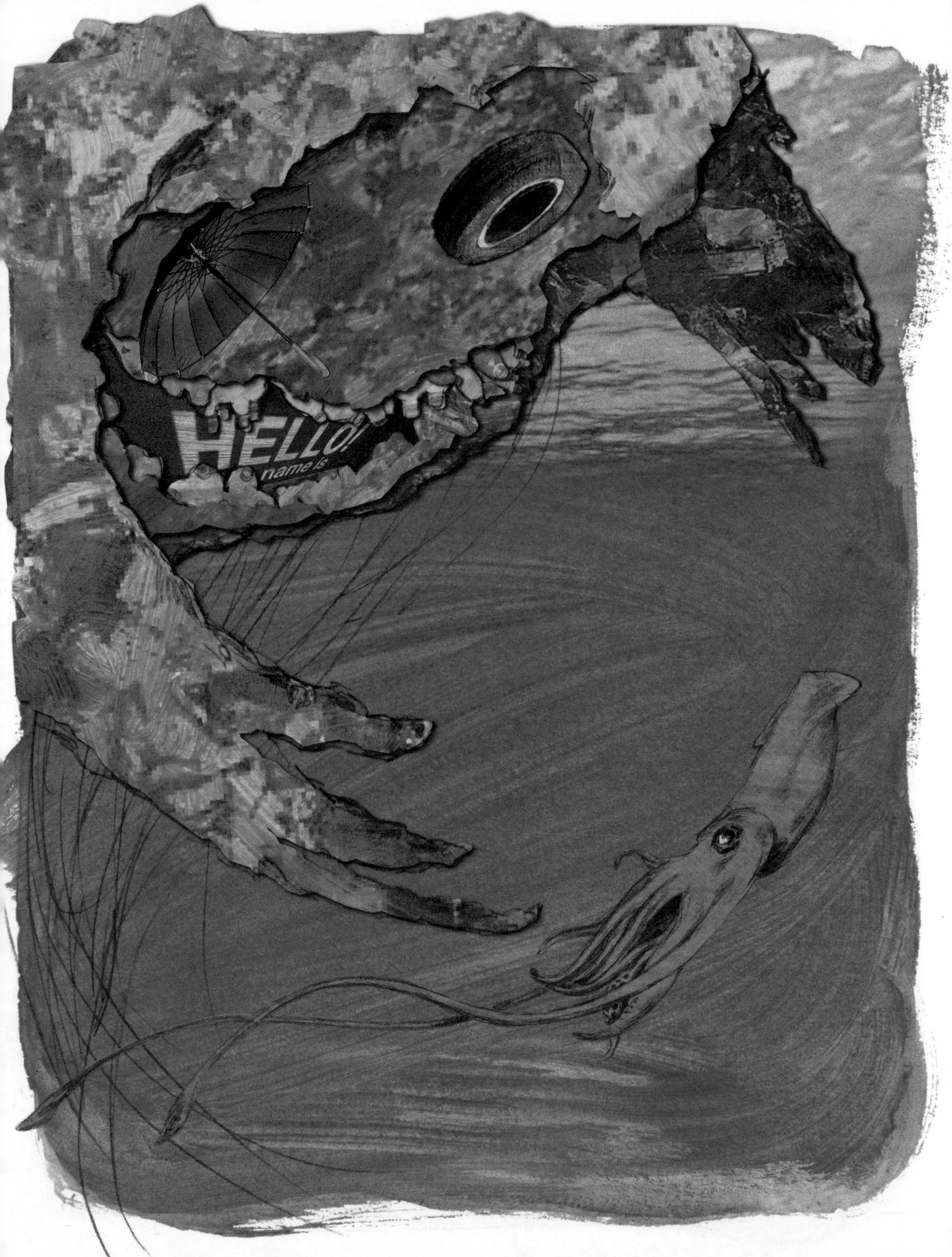
HELLO!
name is

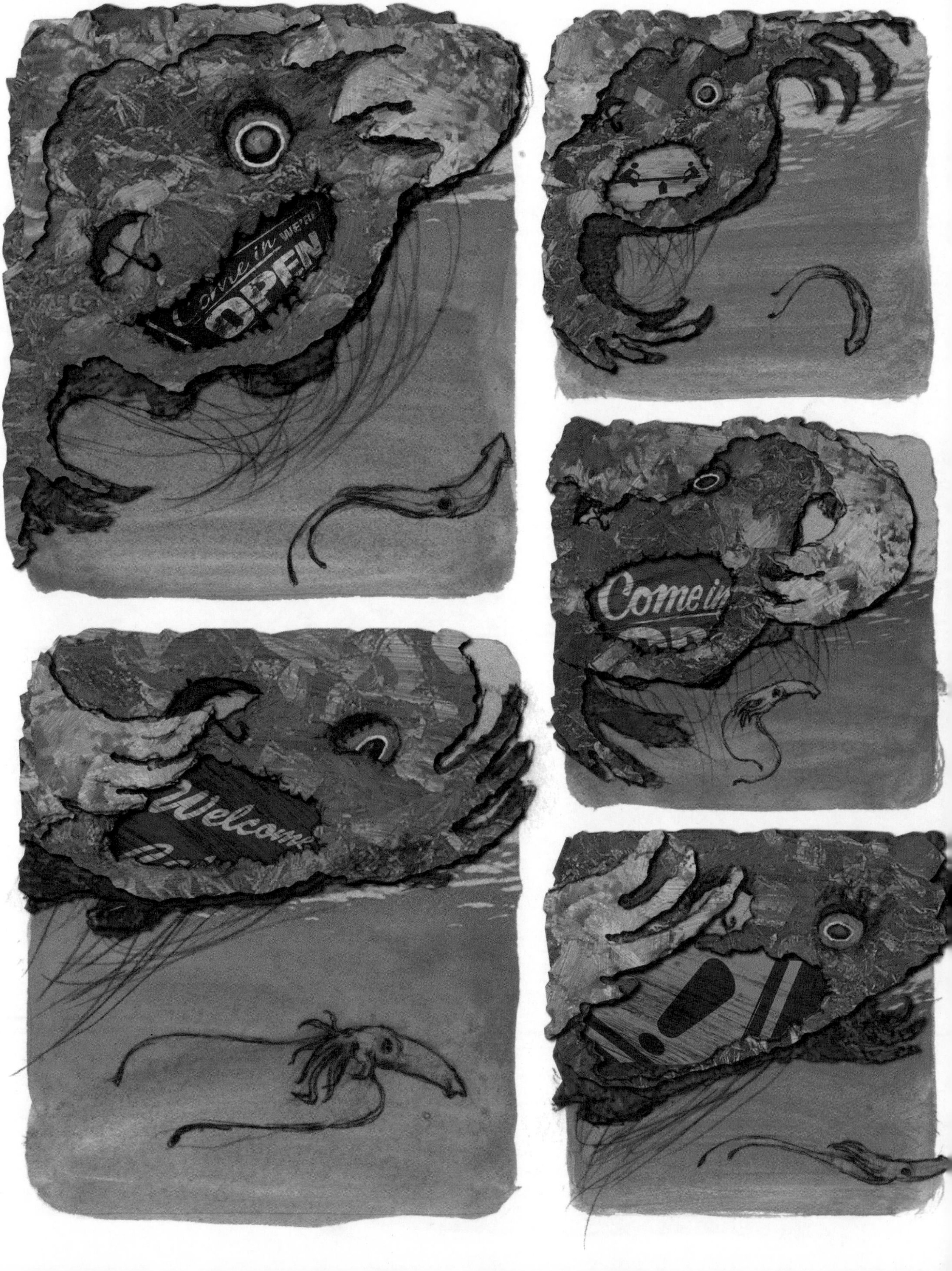
Come in WE'RE
OPEN
Come in
Welcom

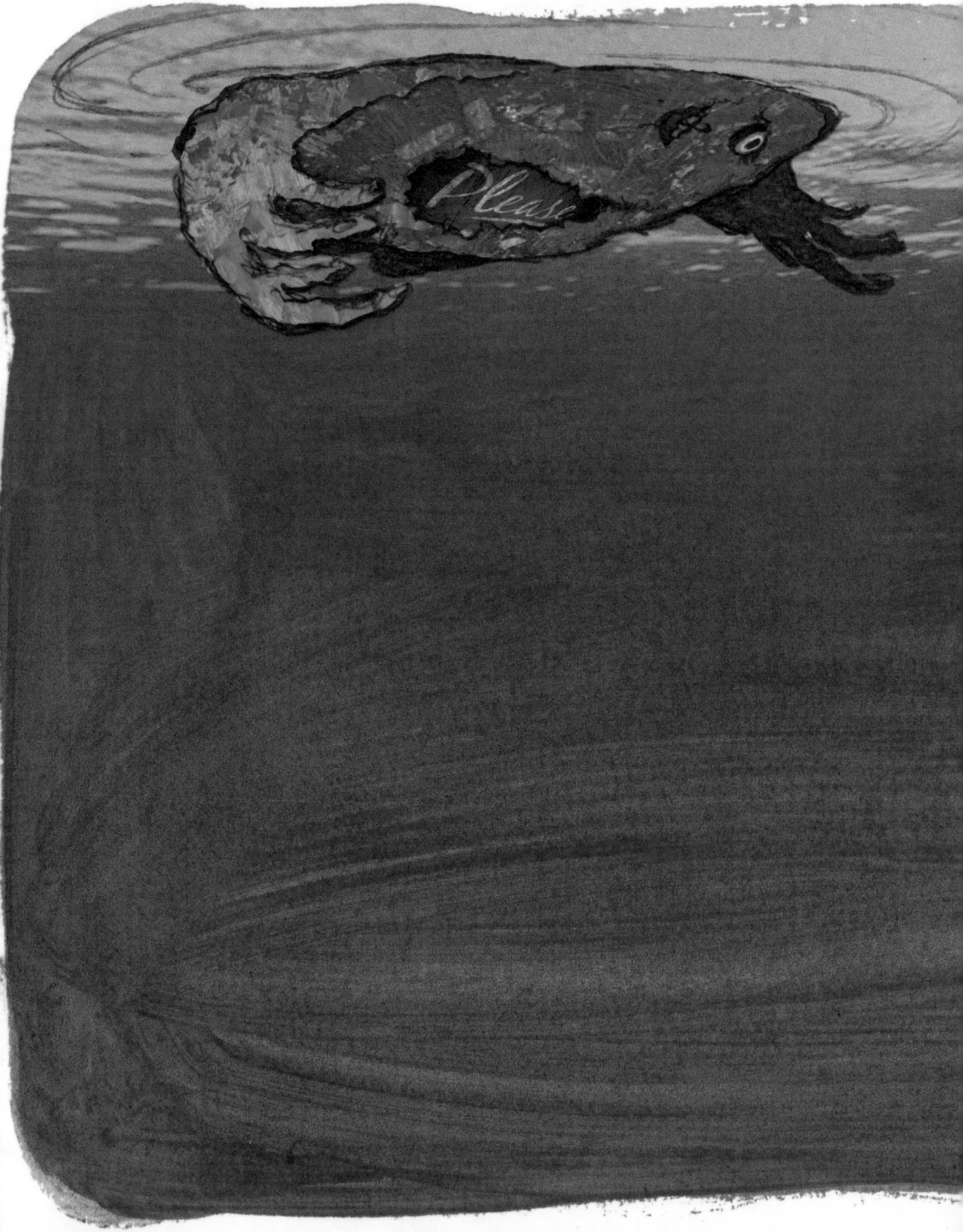
Please

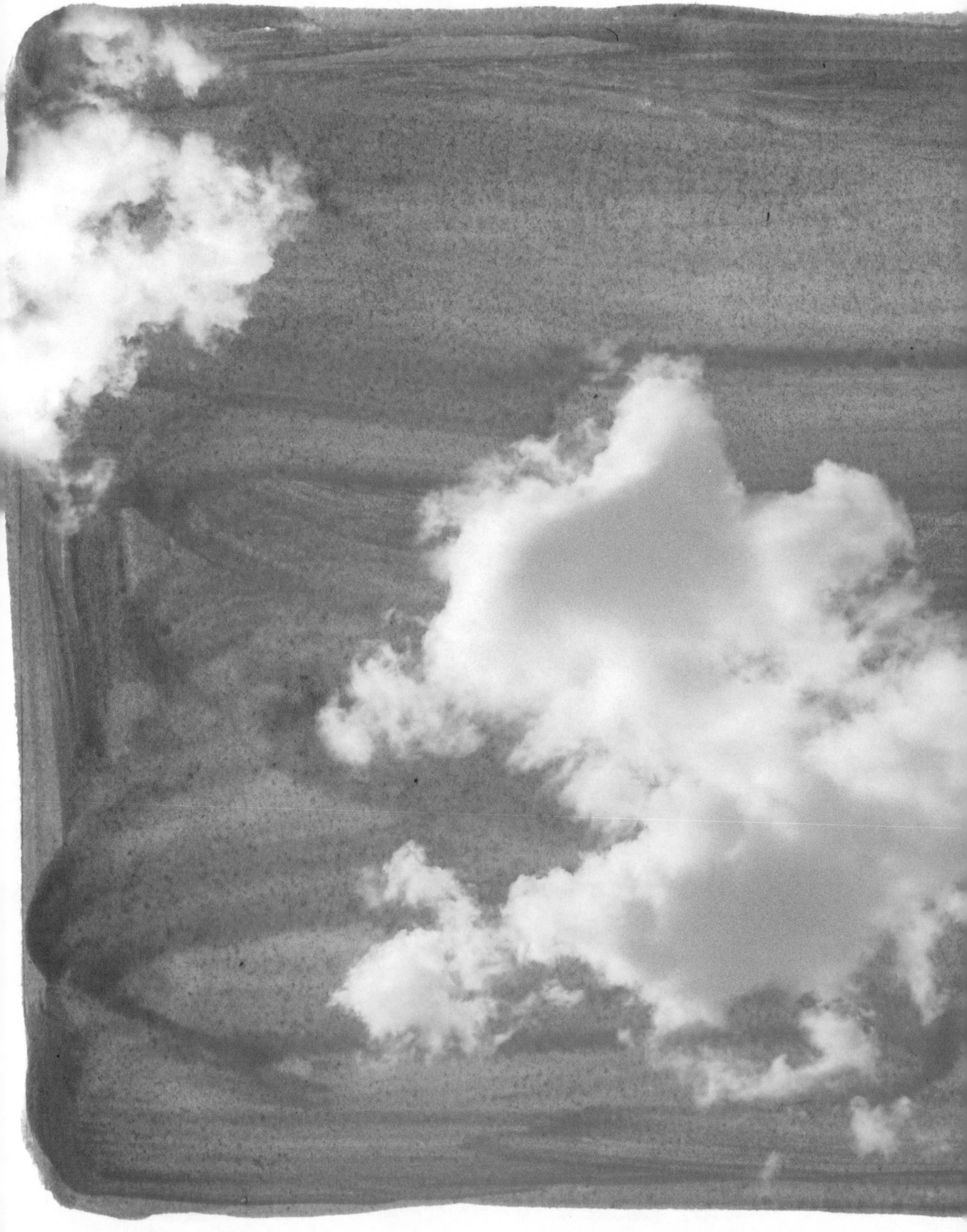

# three

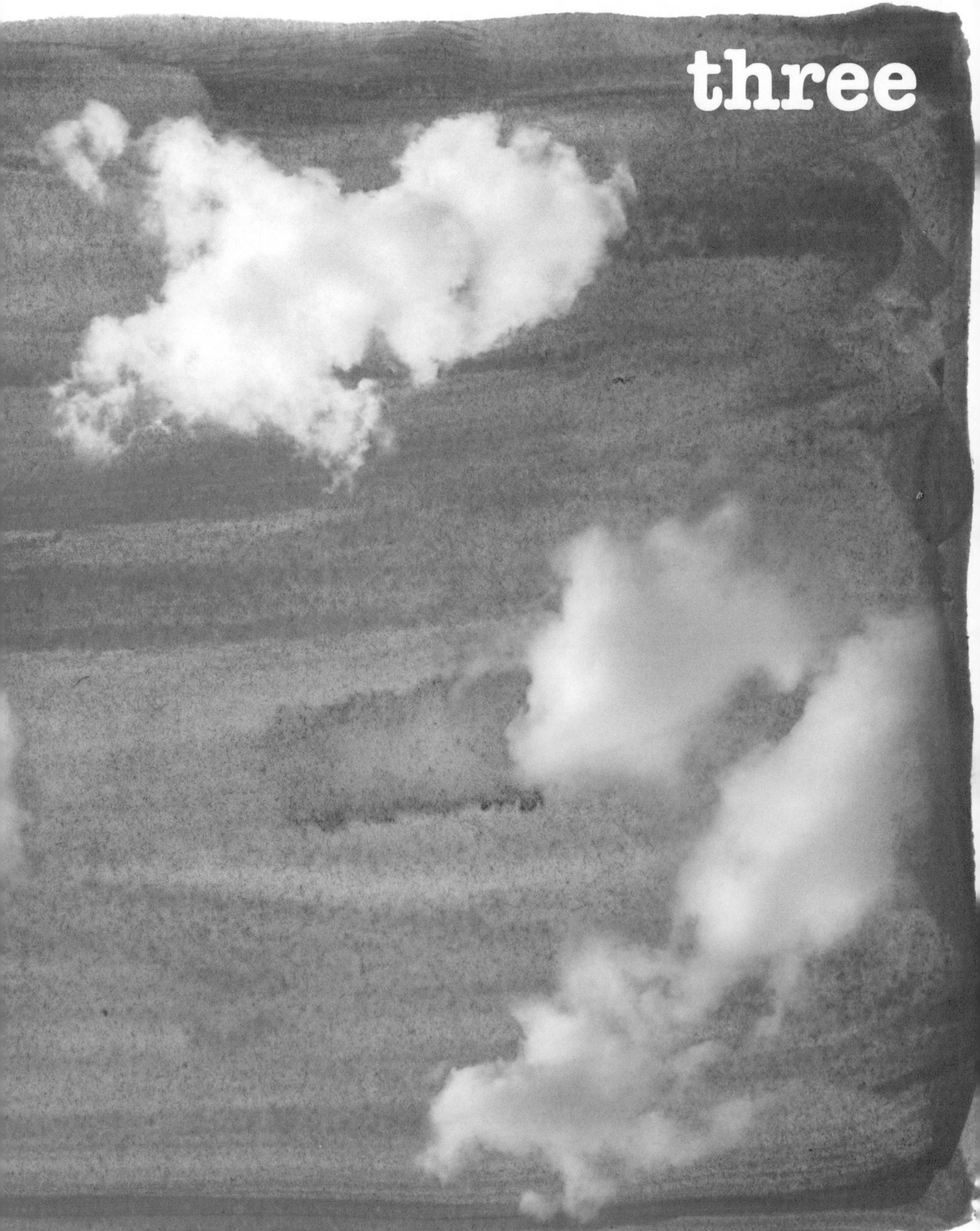

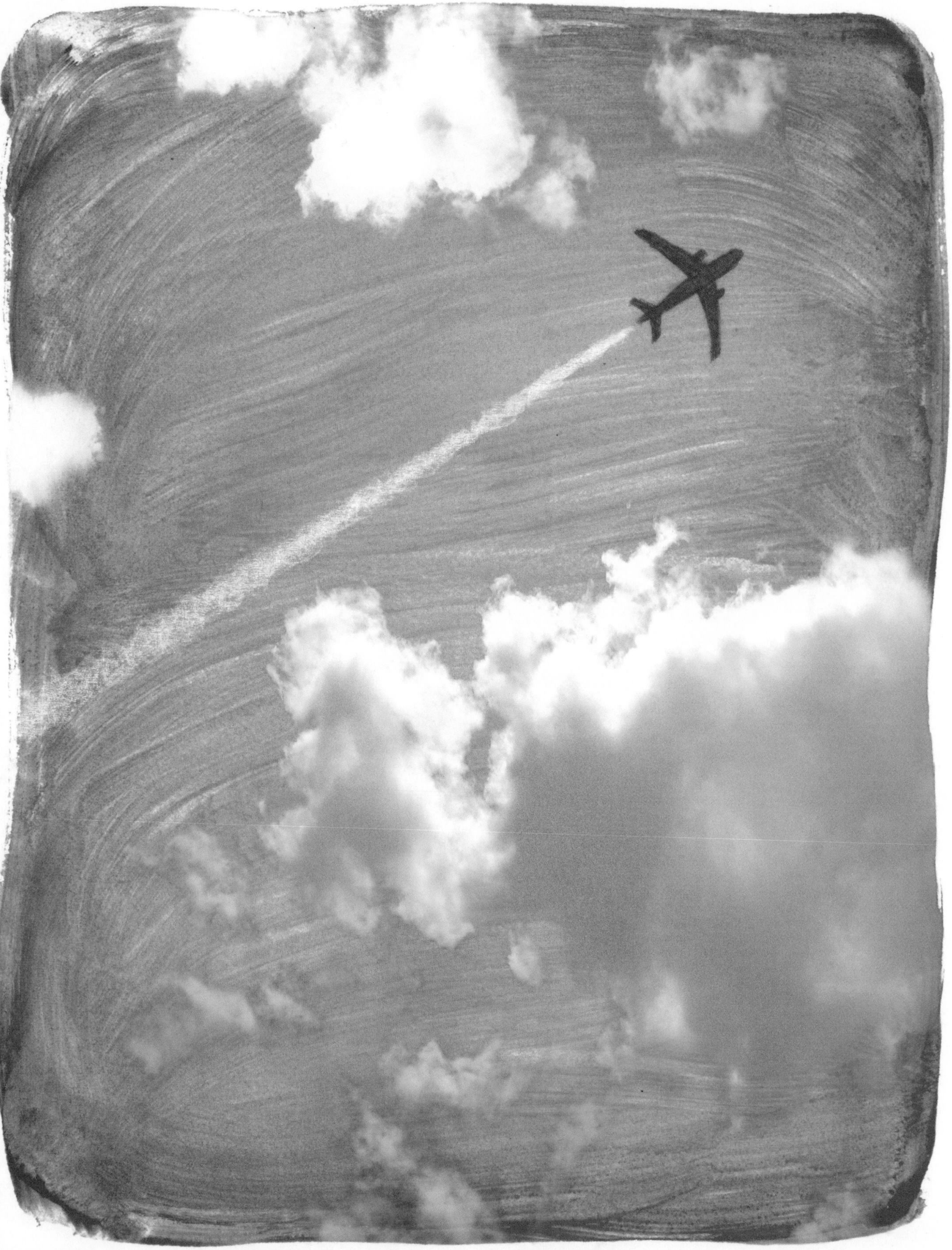

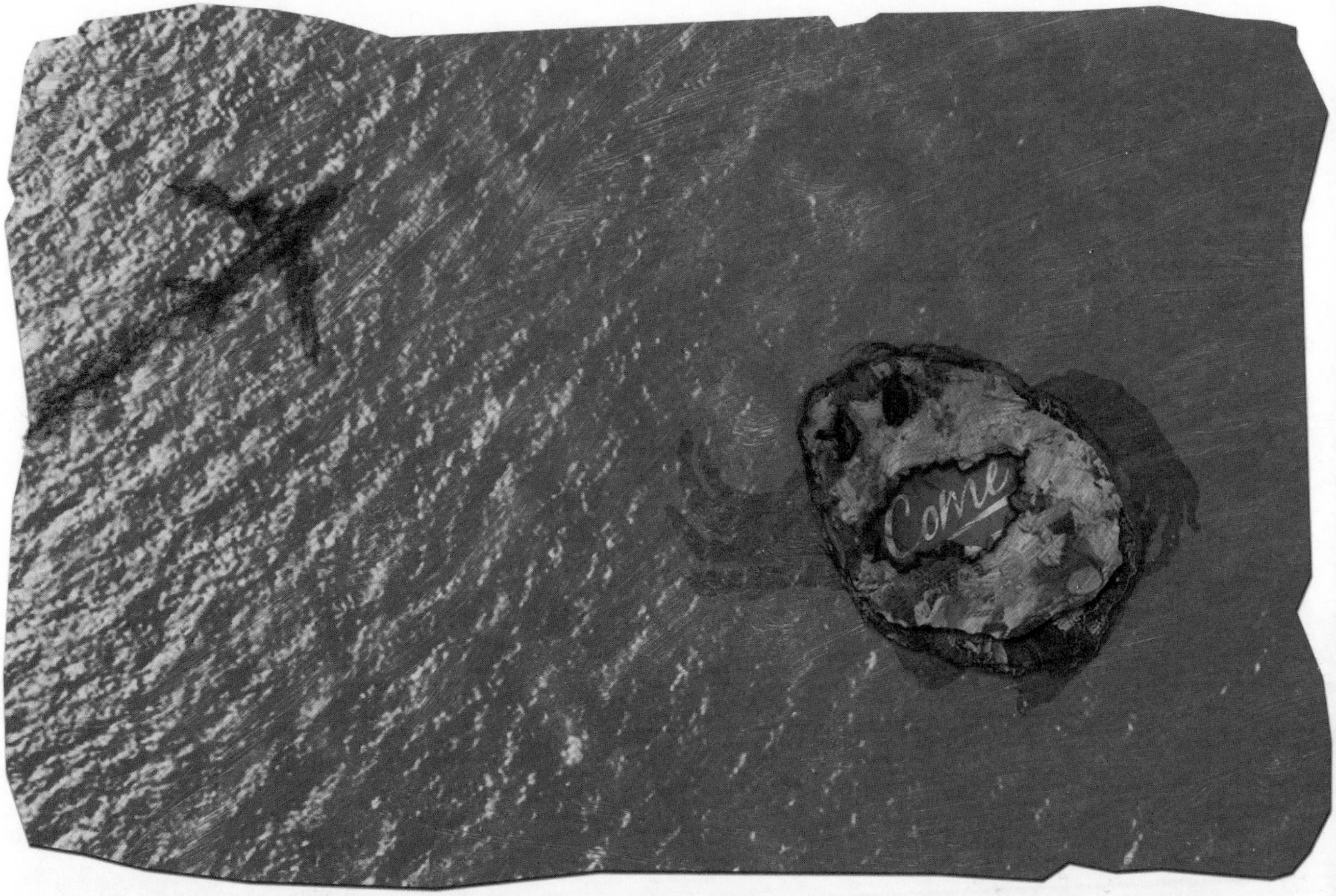
Come

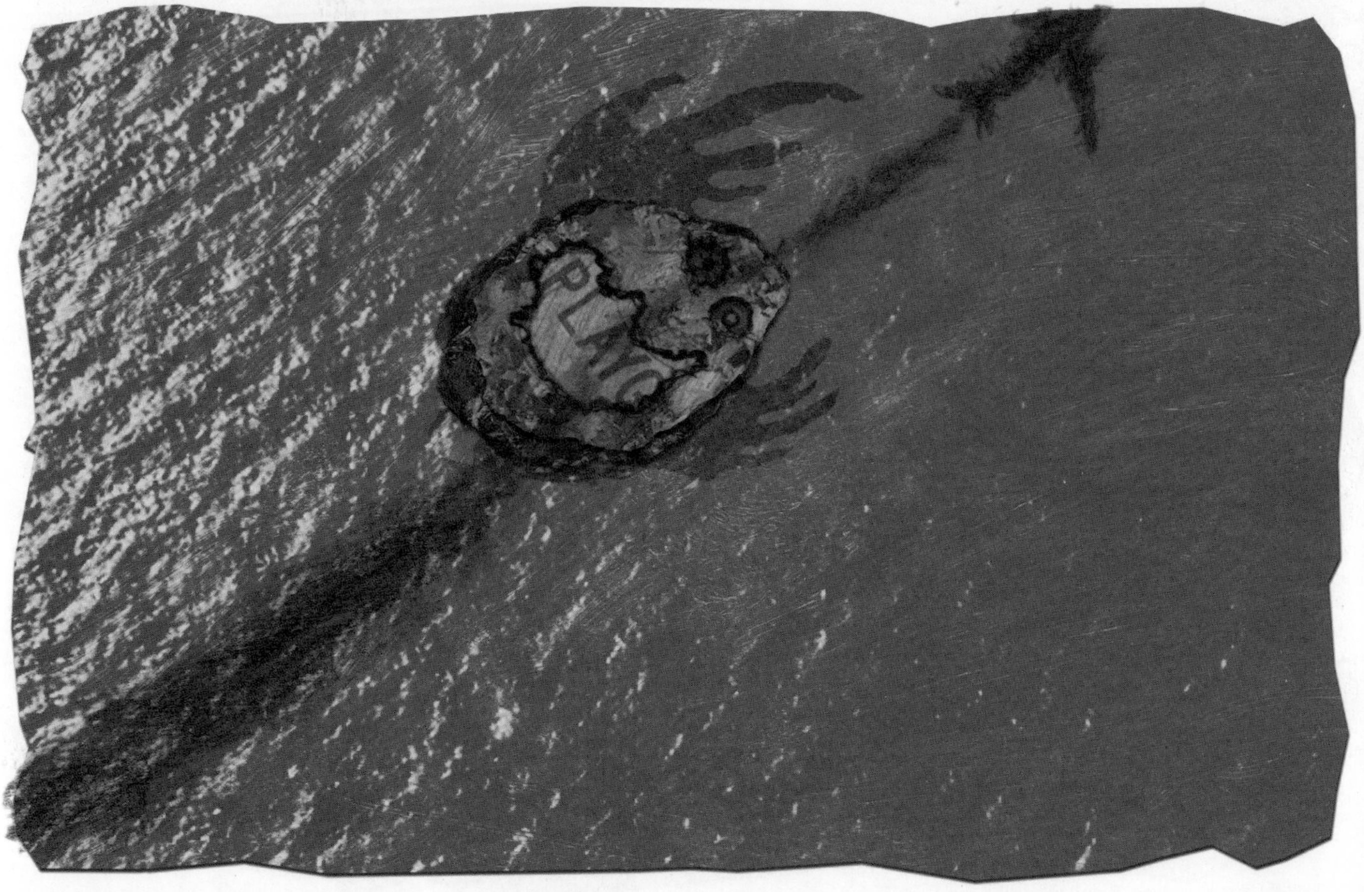

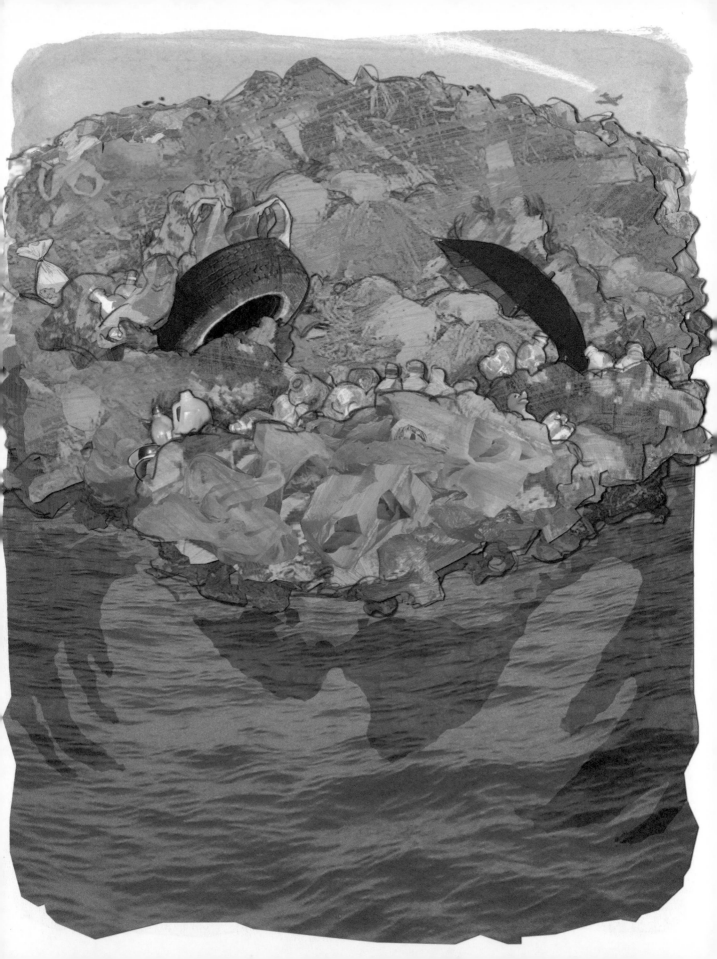

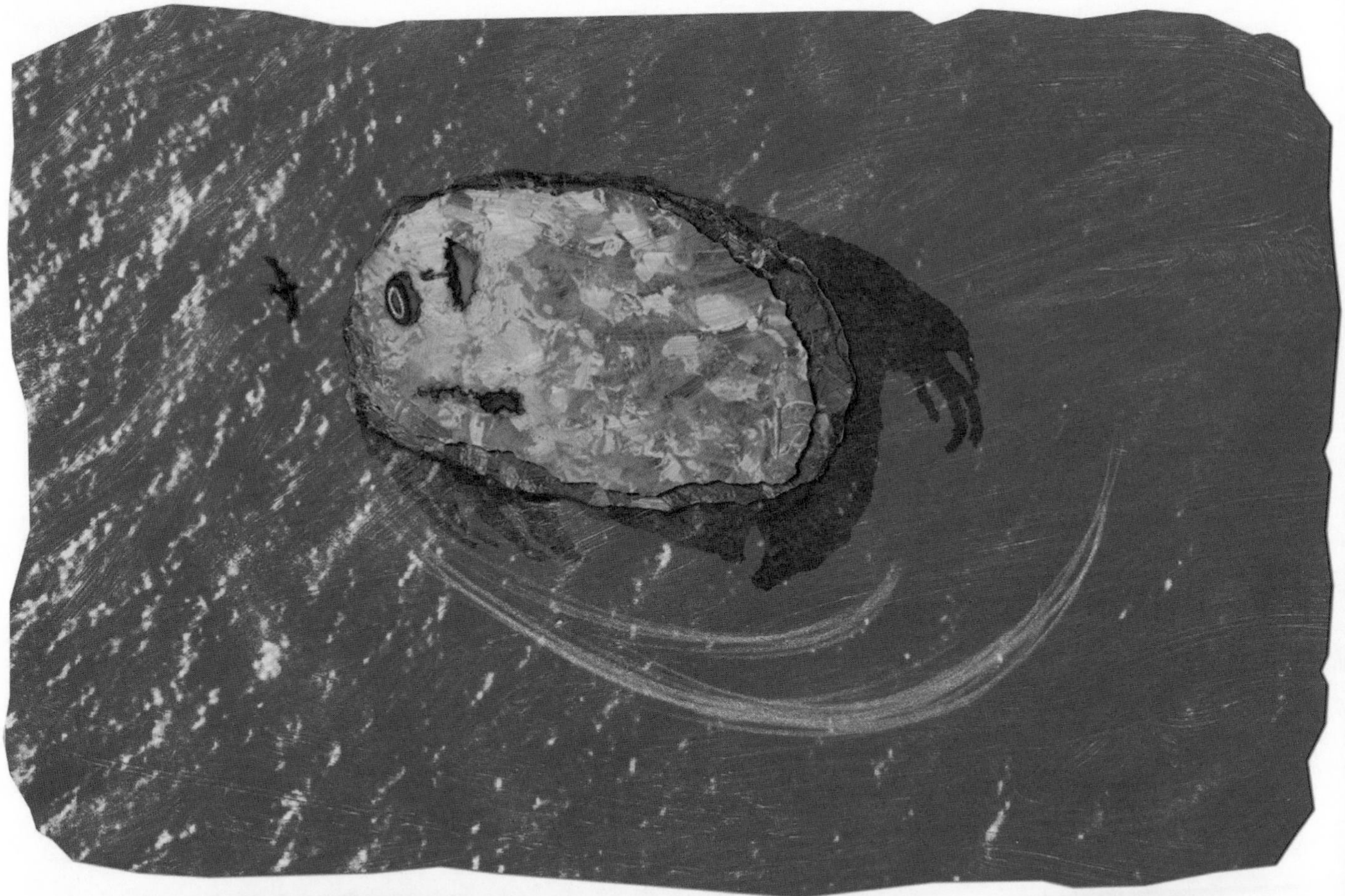

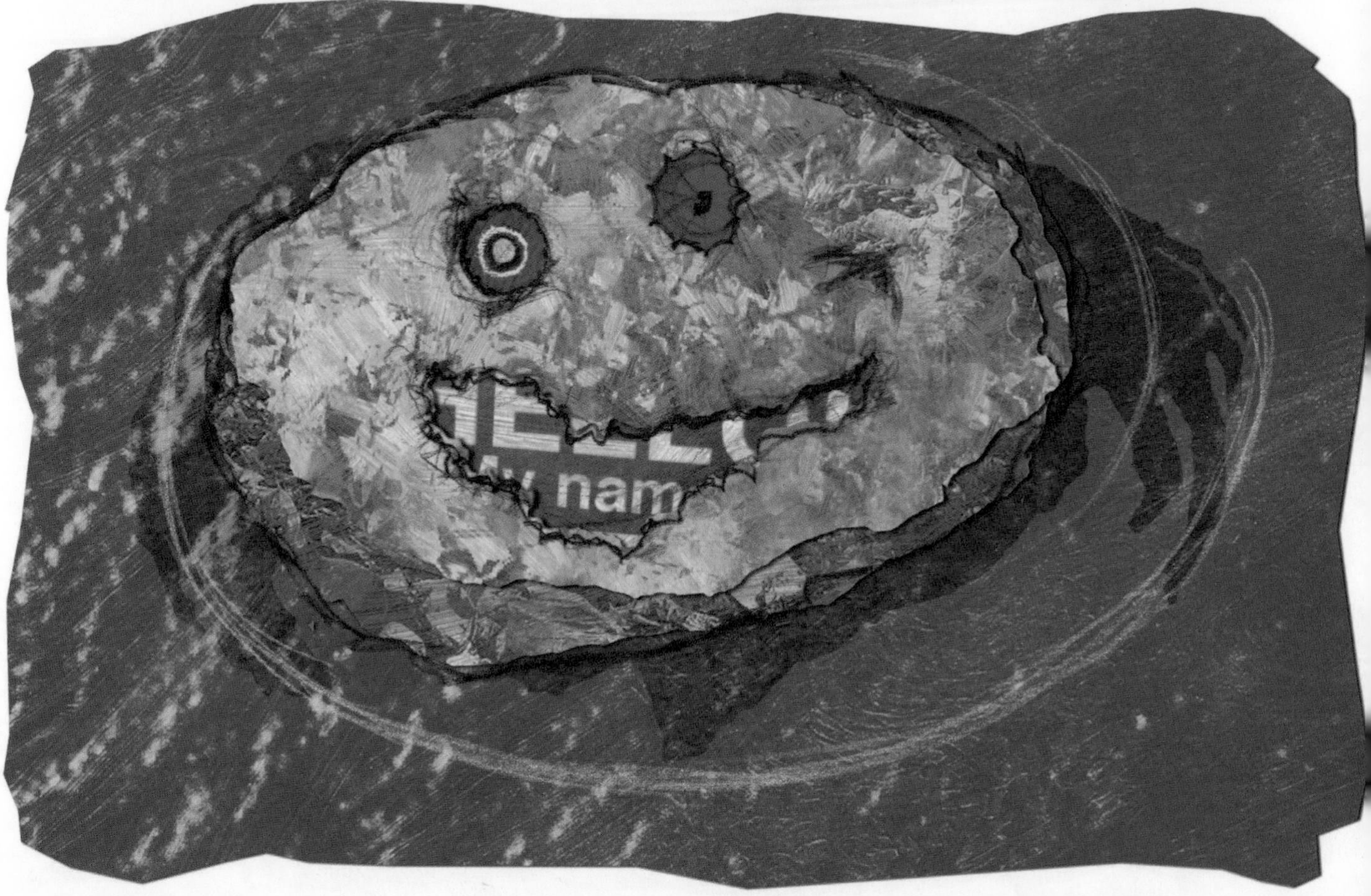

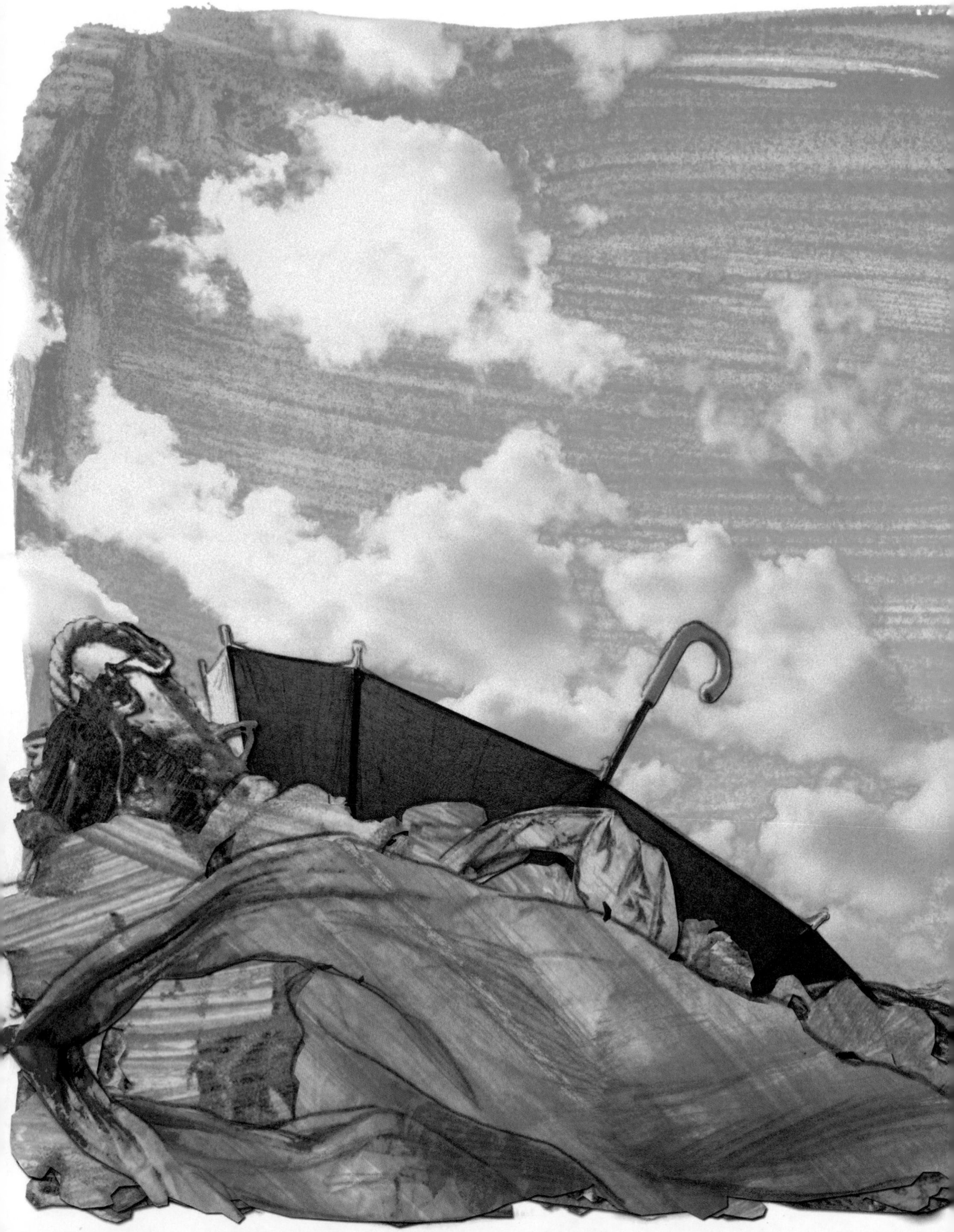

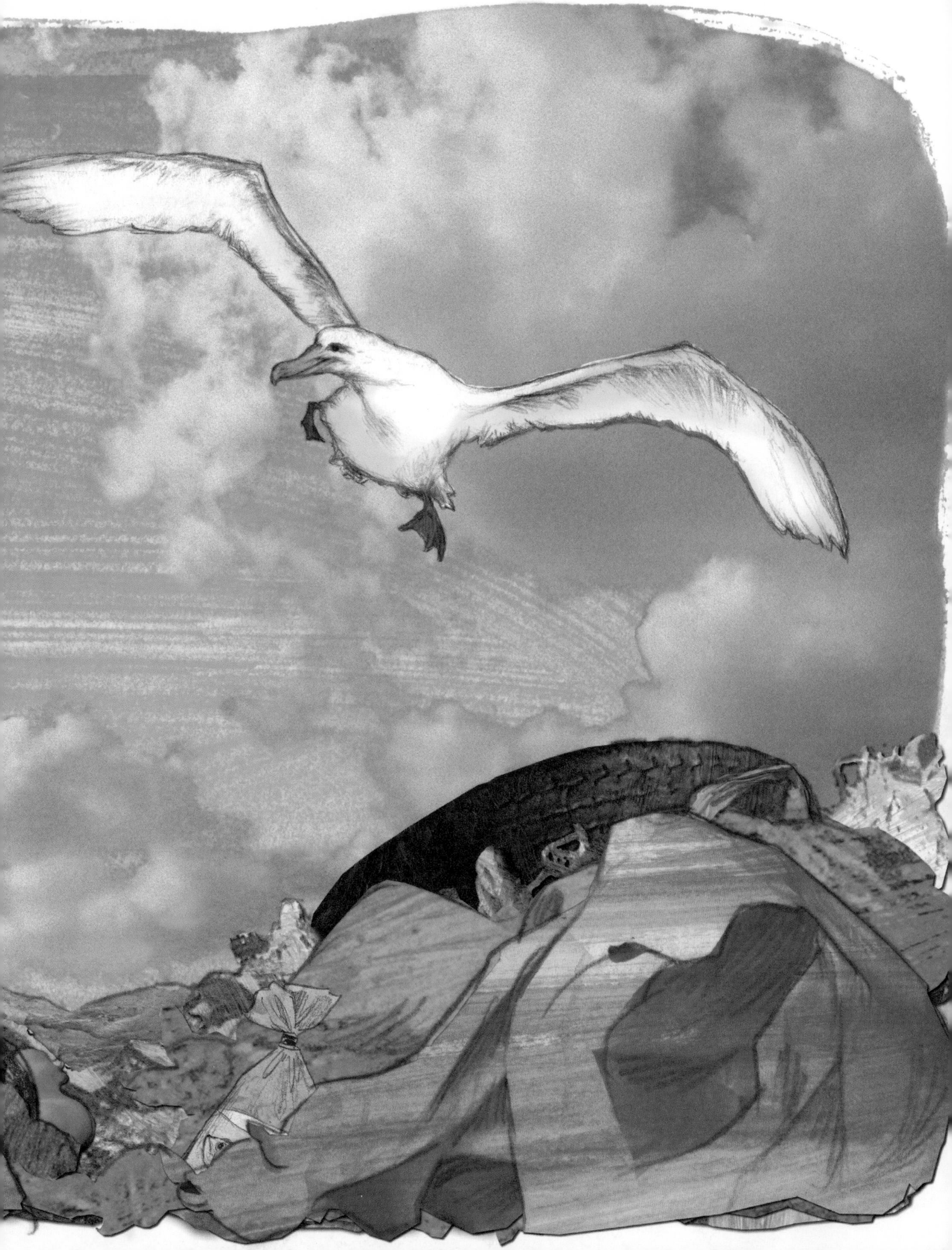

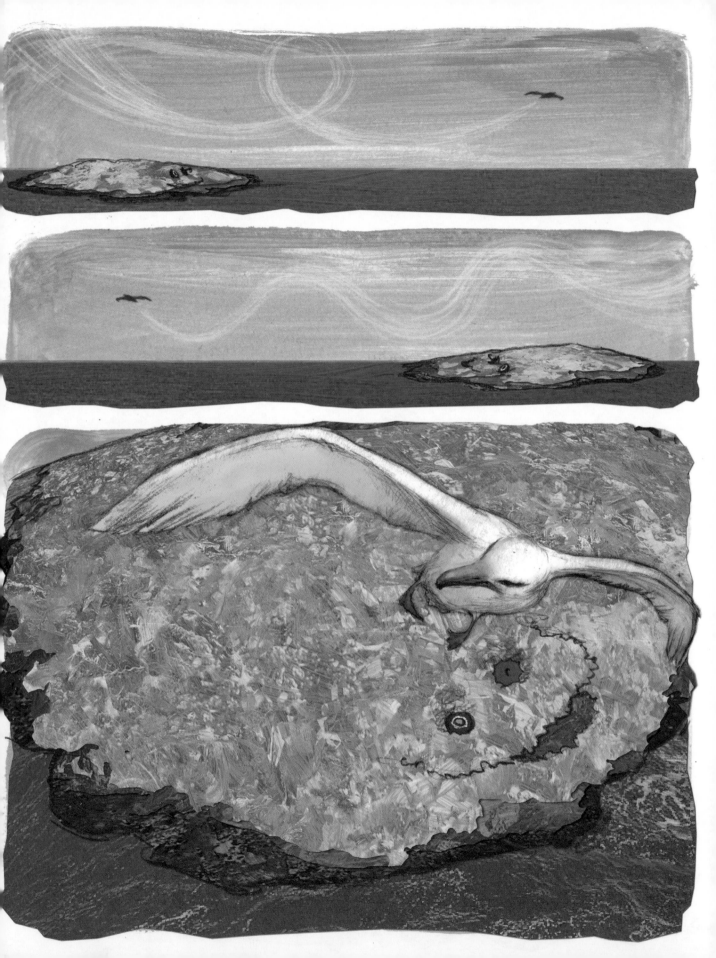

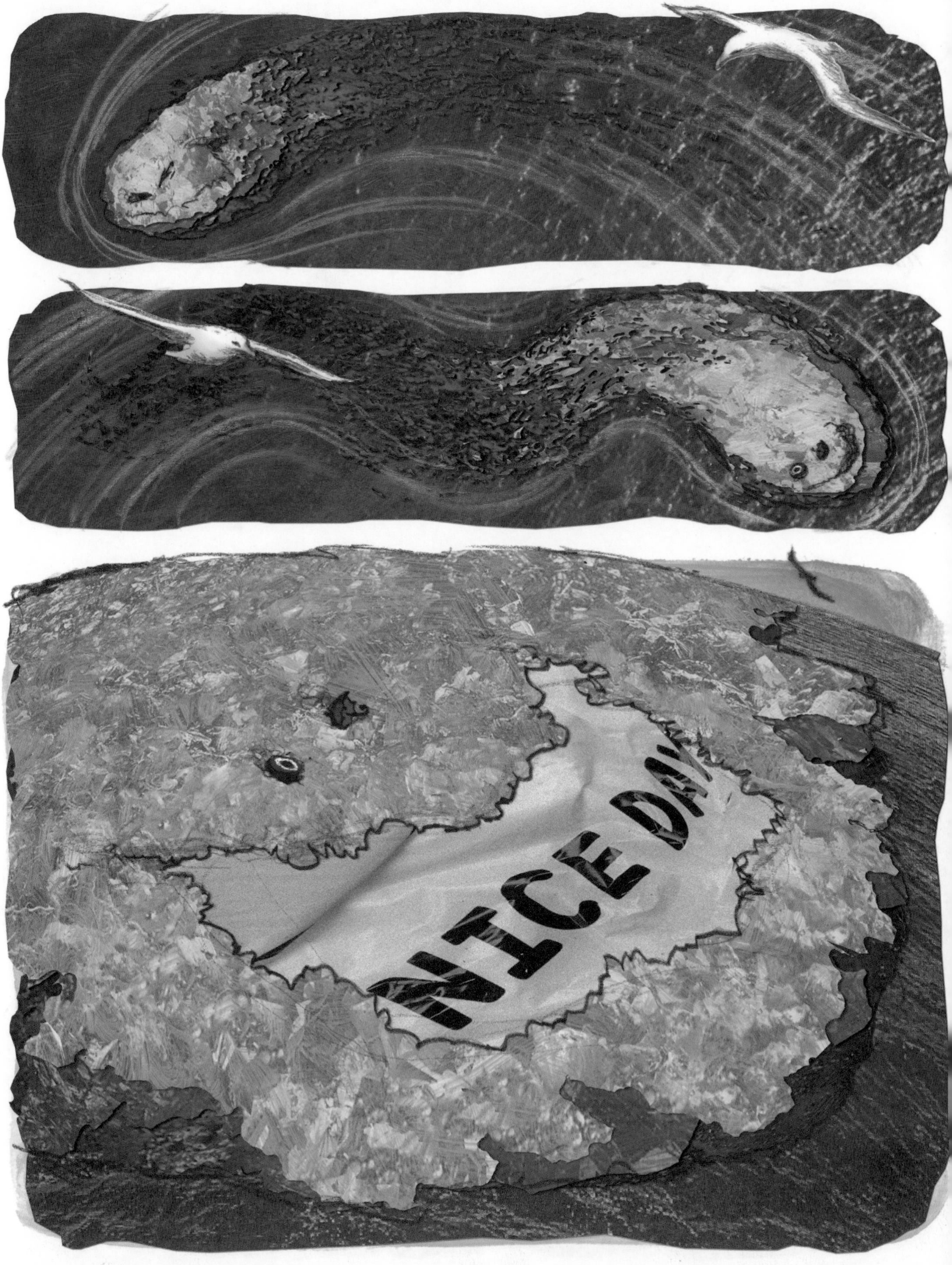
NICE DA

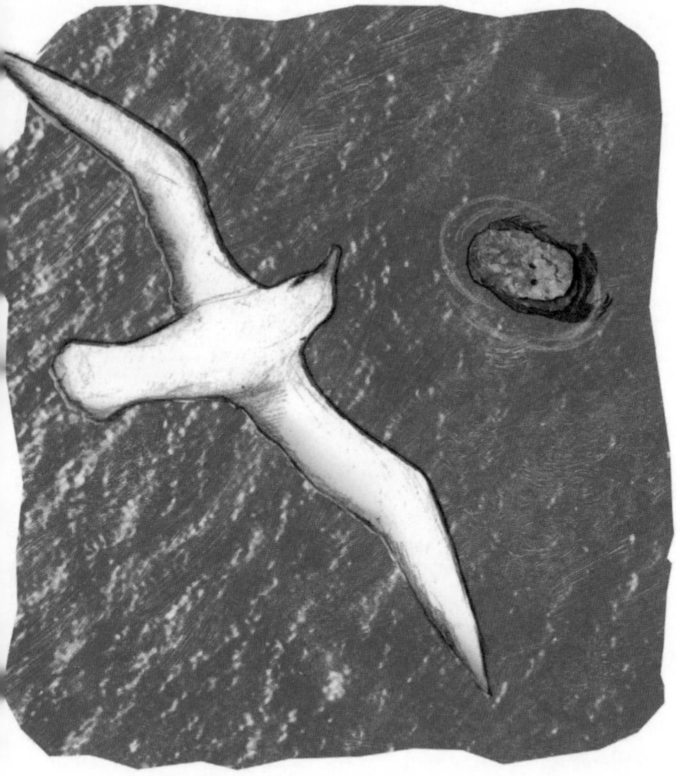
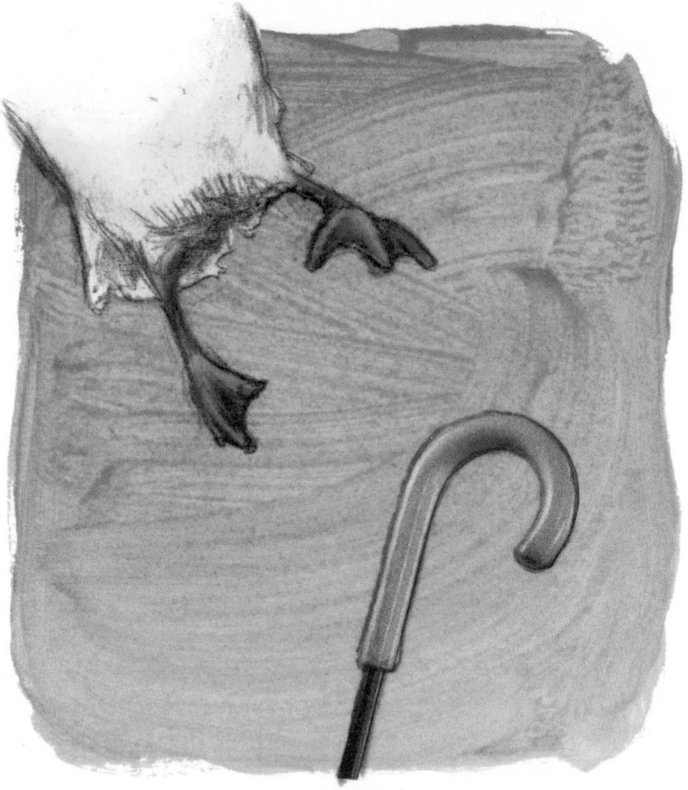
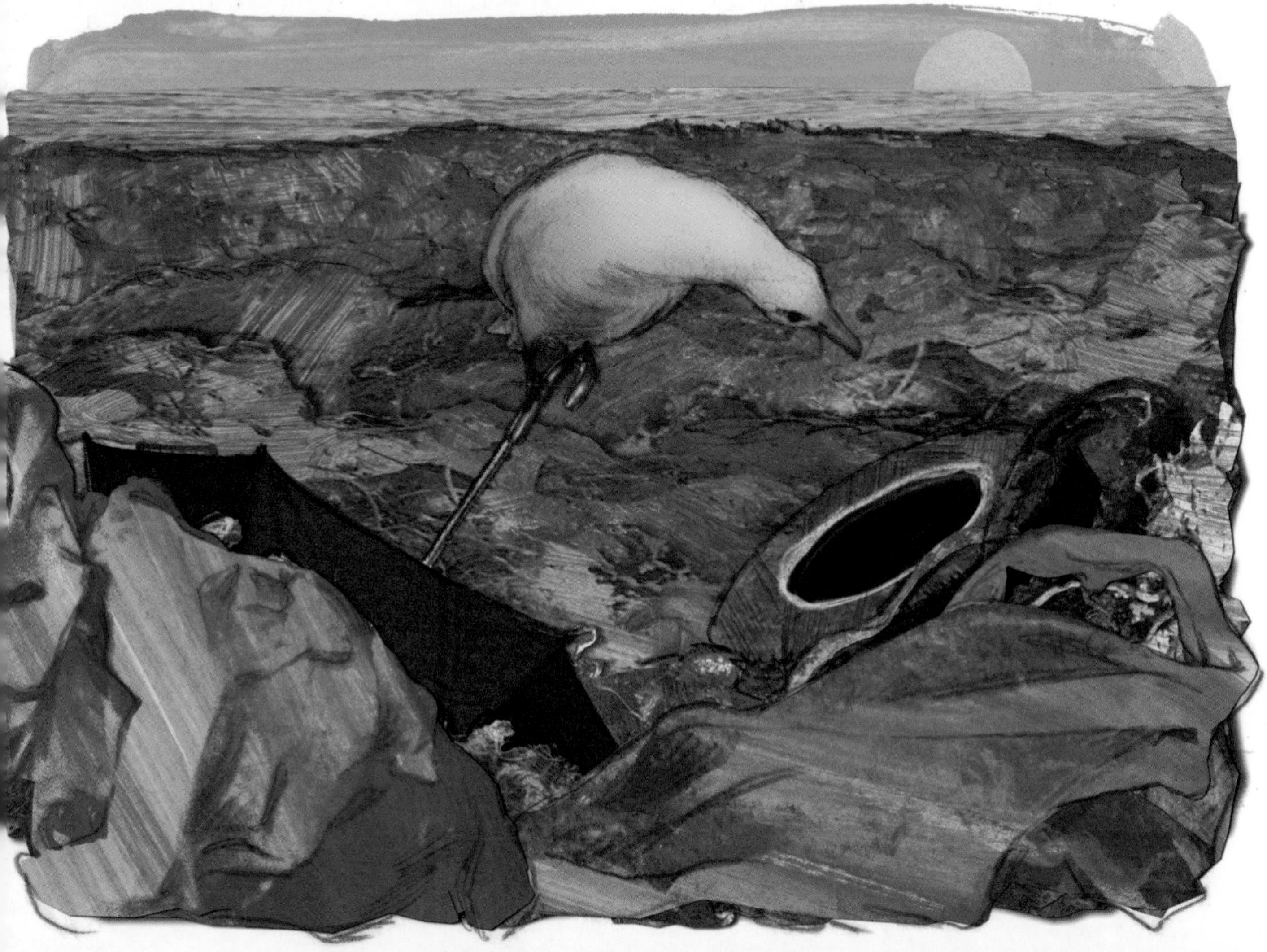

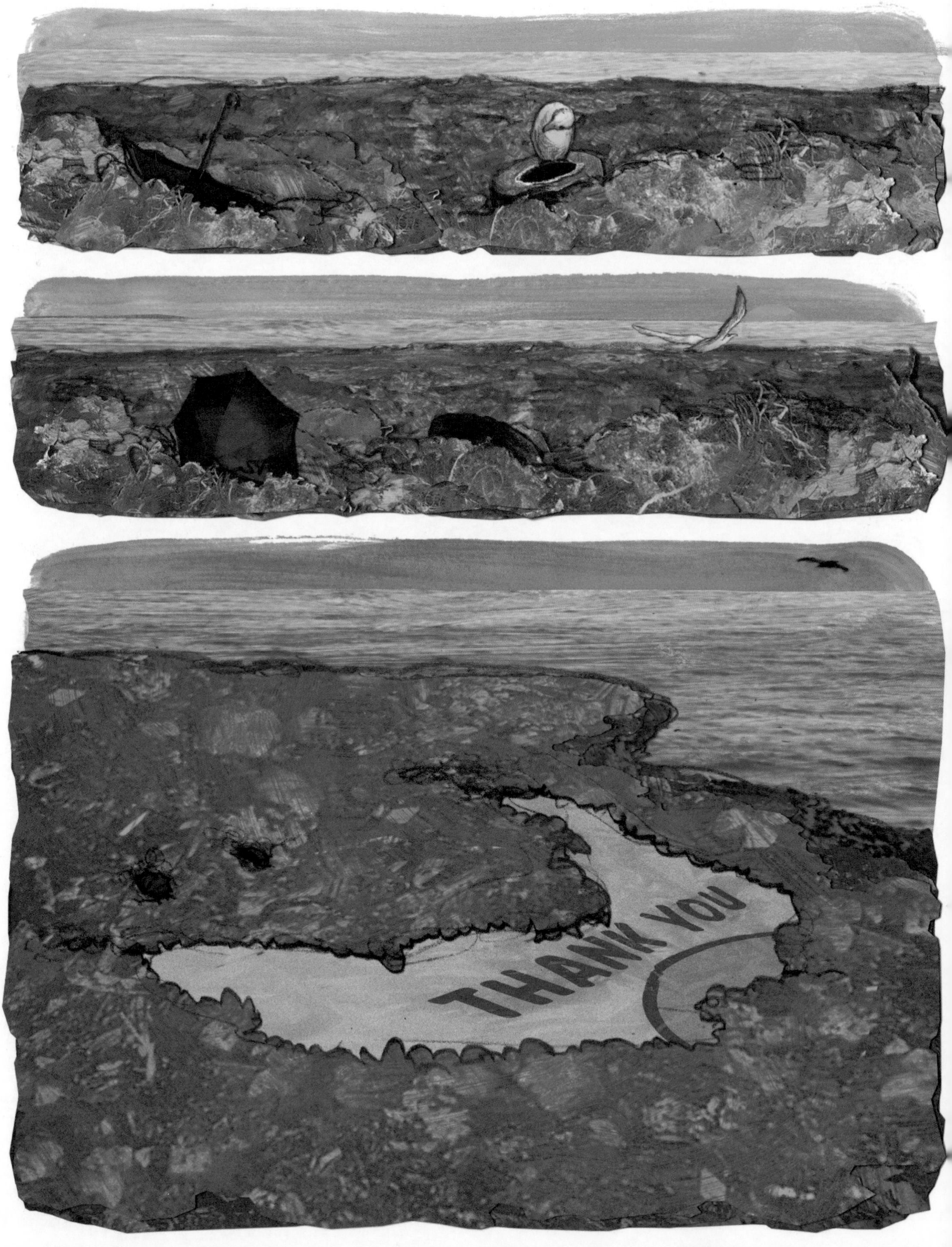
THANK YOU

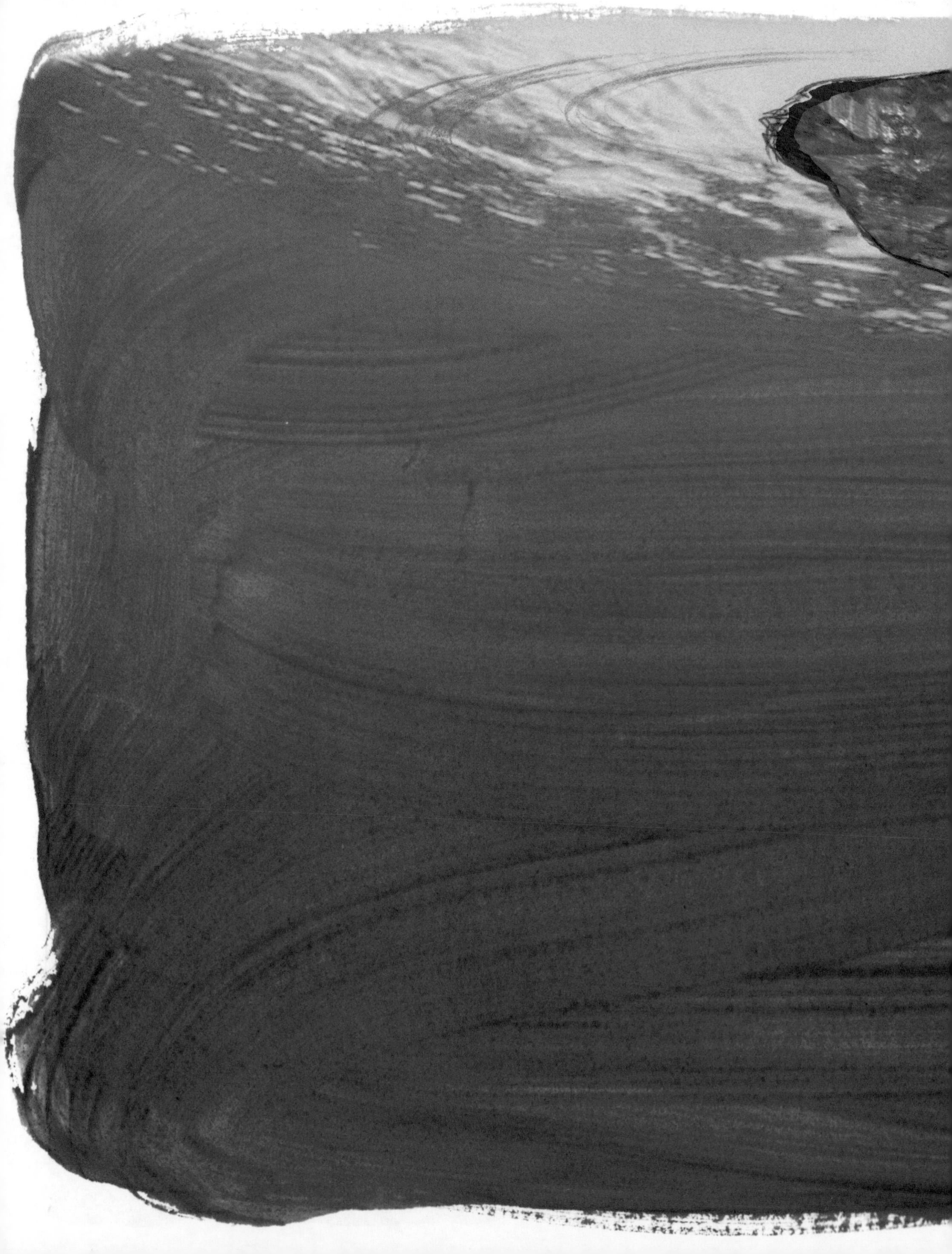

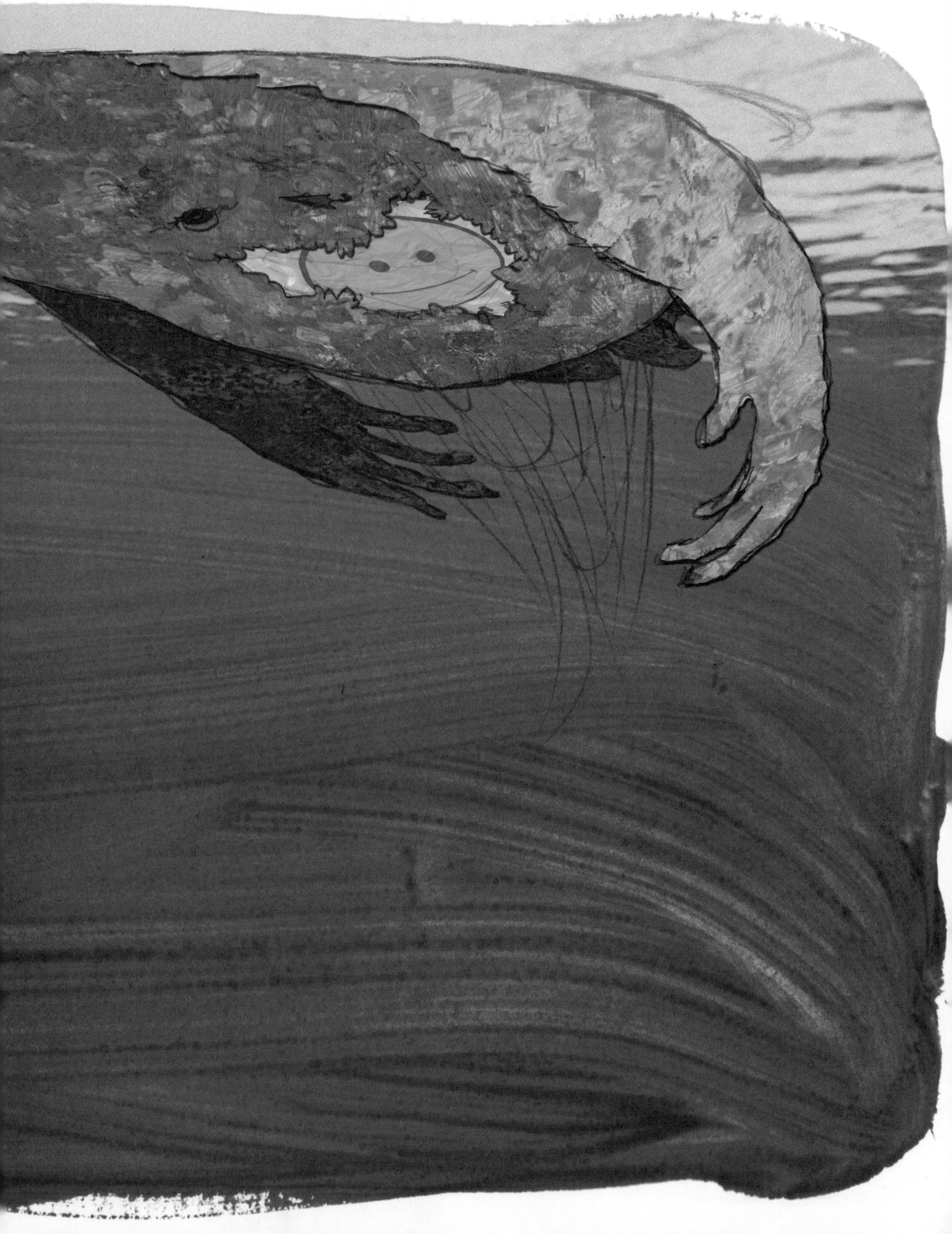

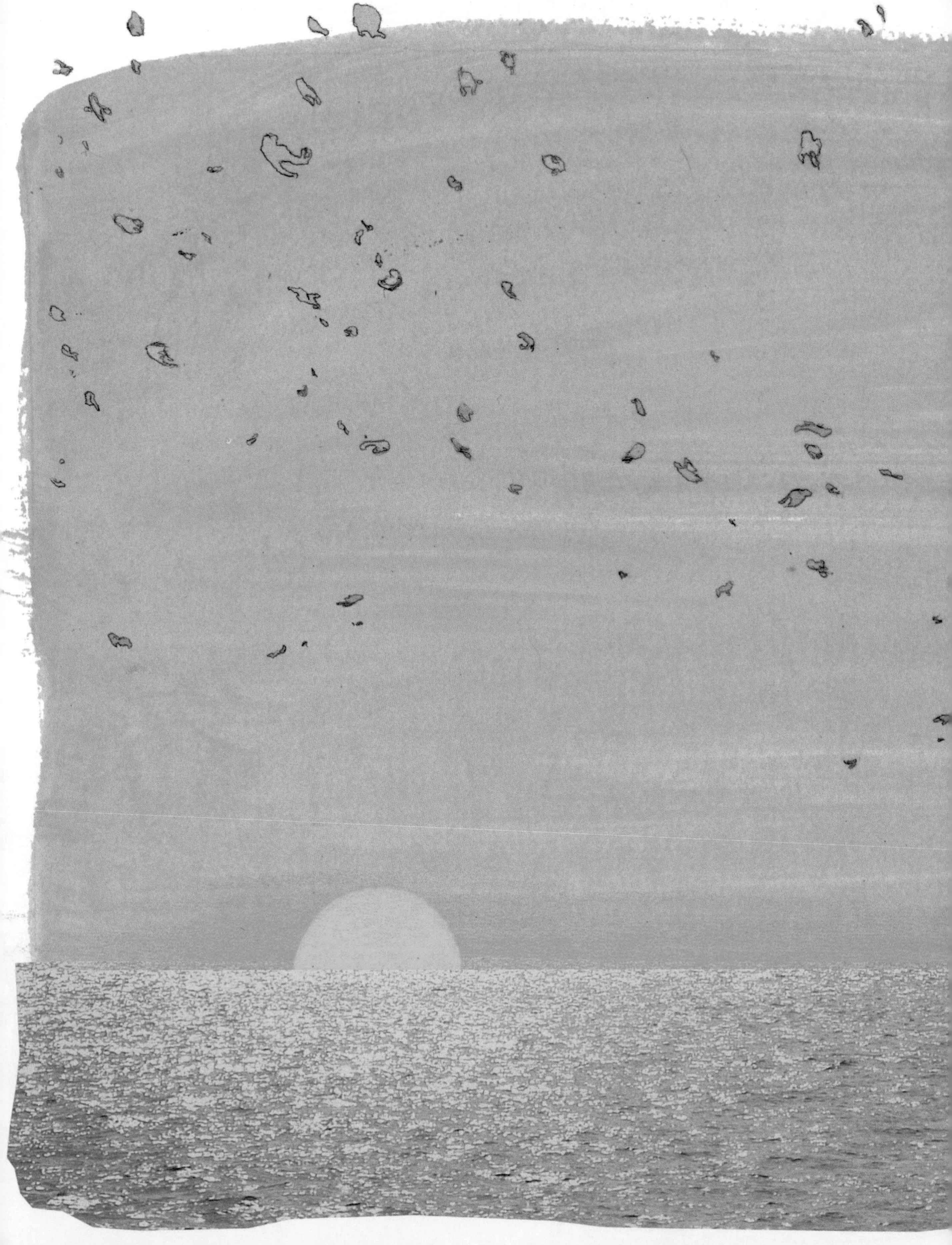

# four

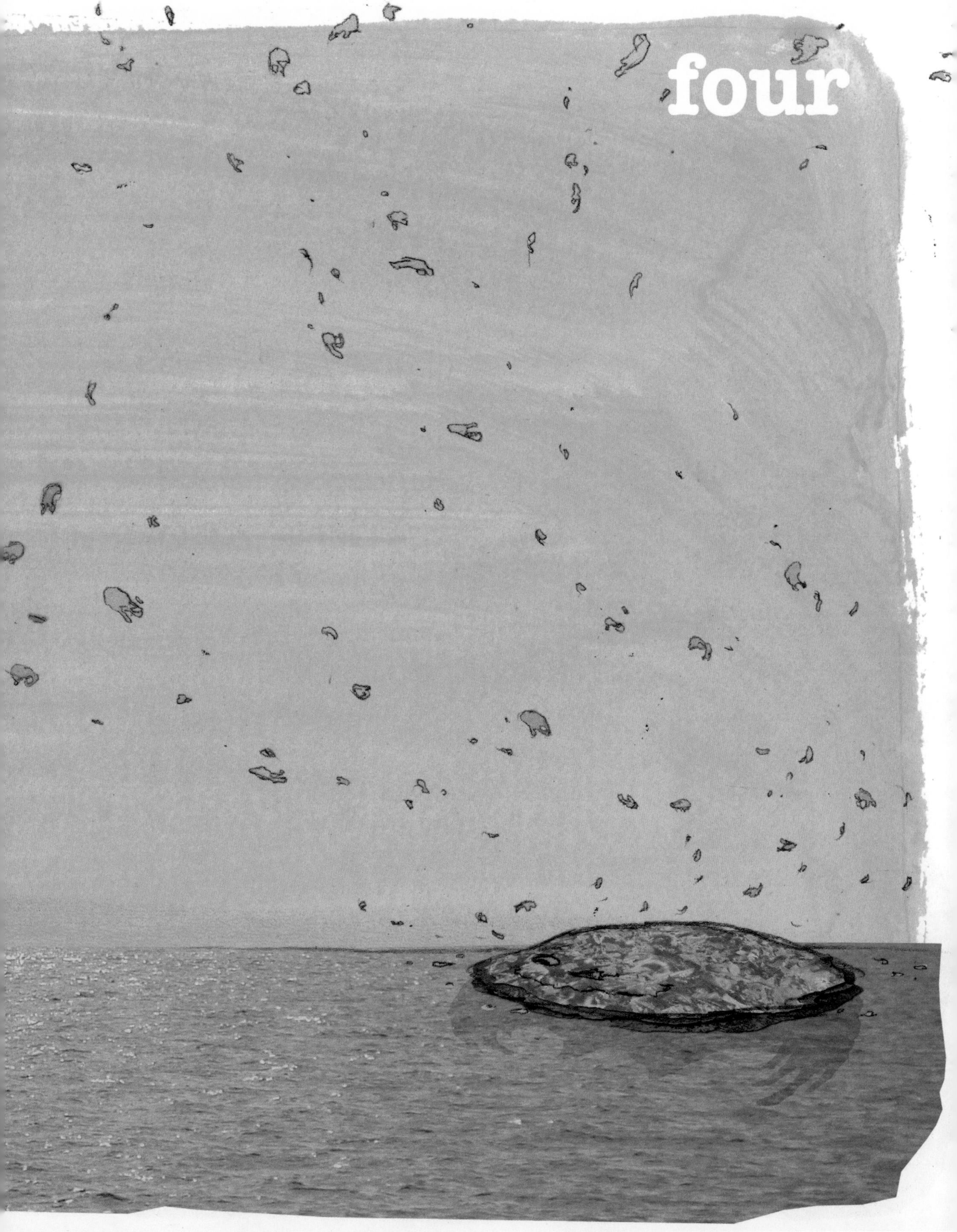

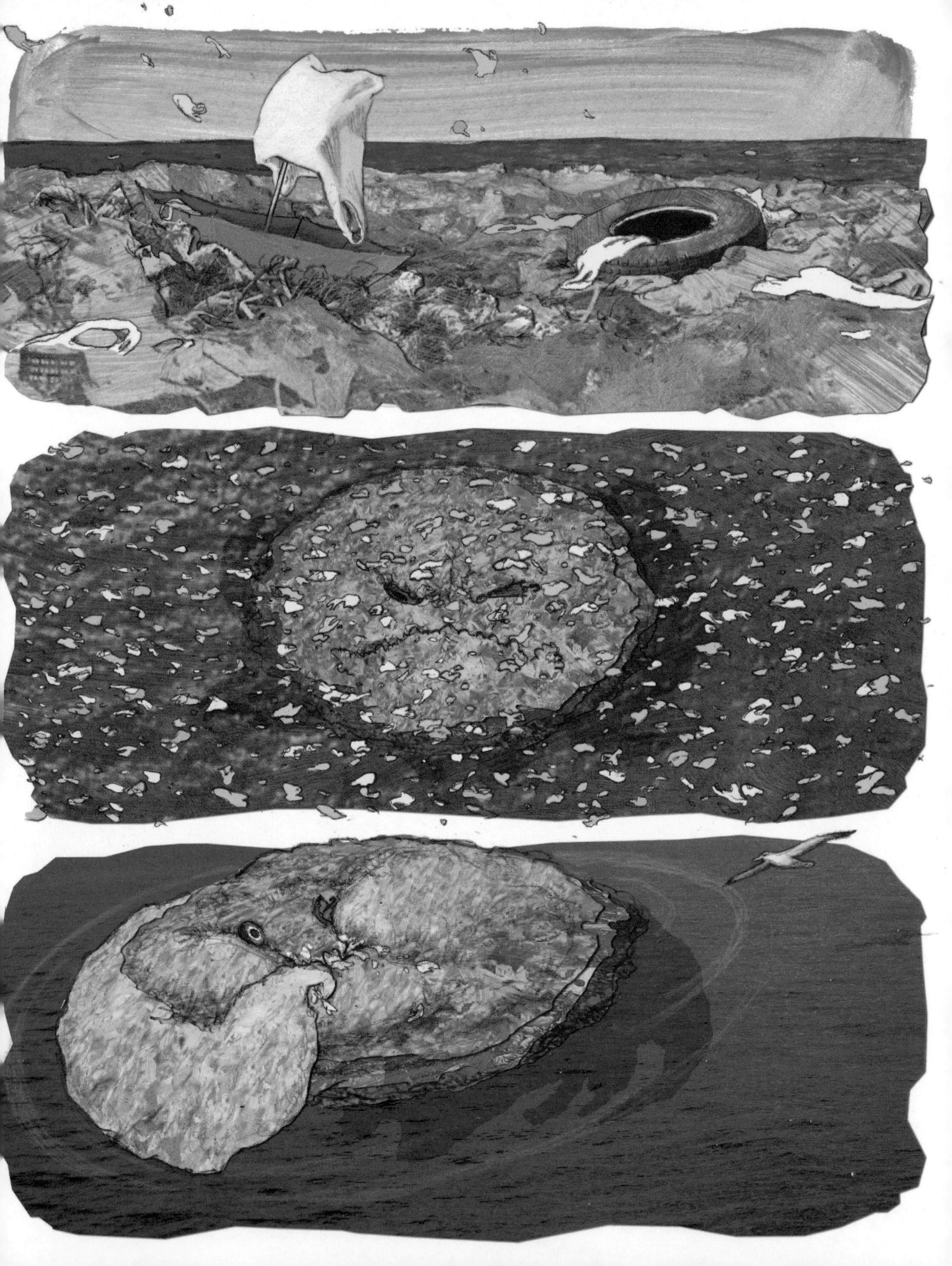

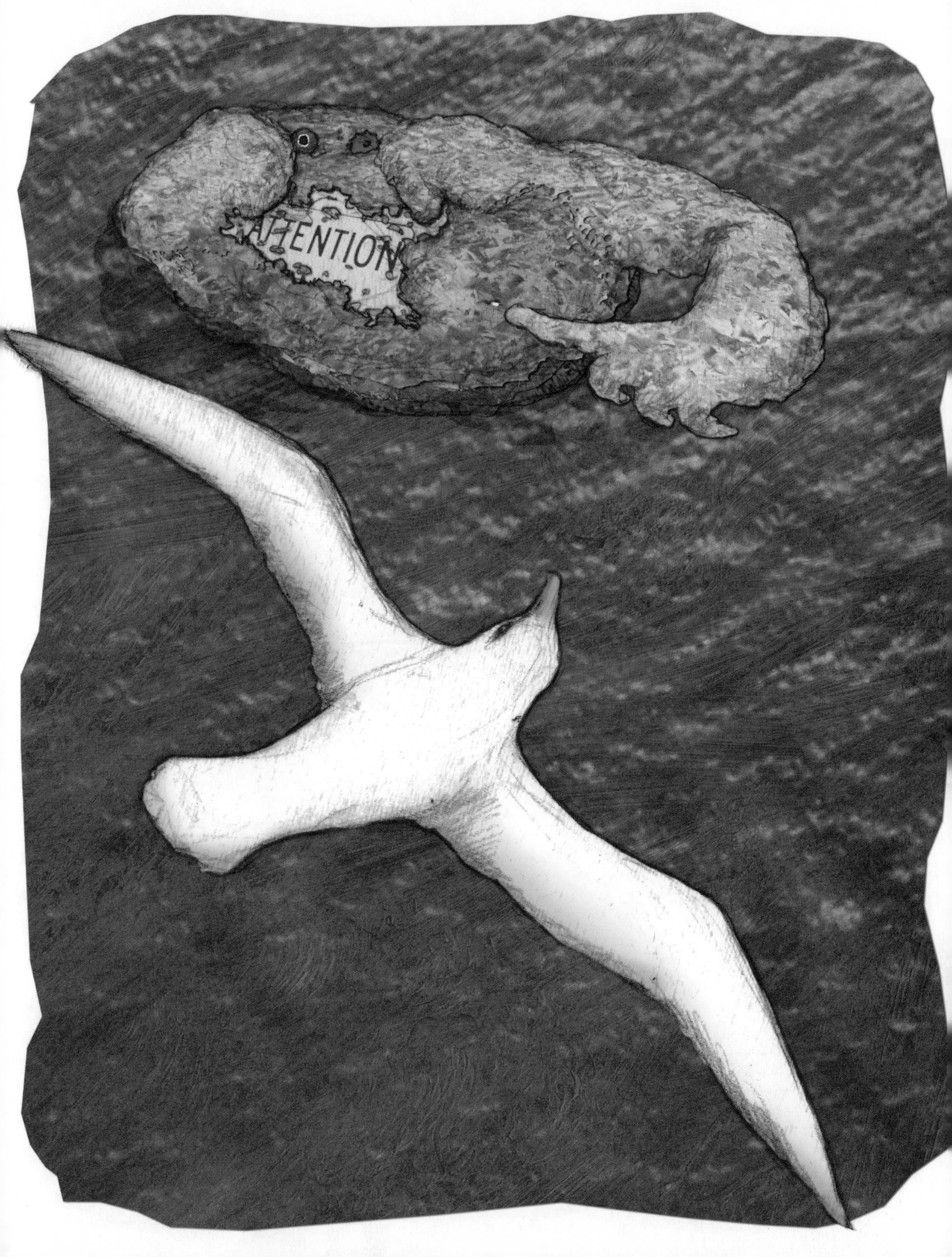
ATTENTION

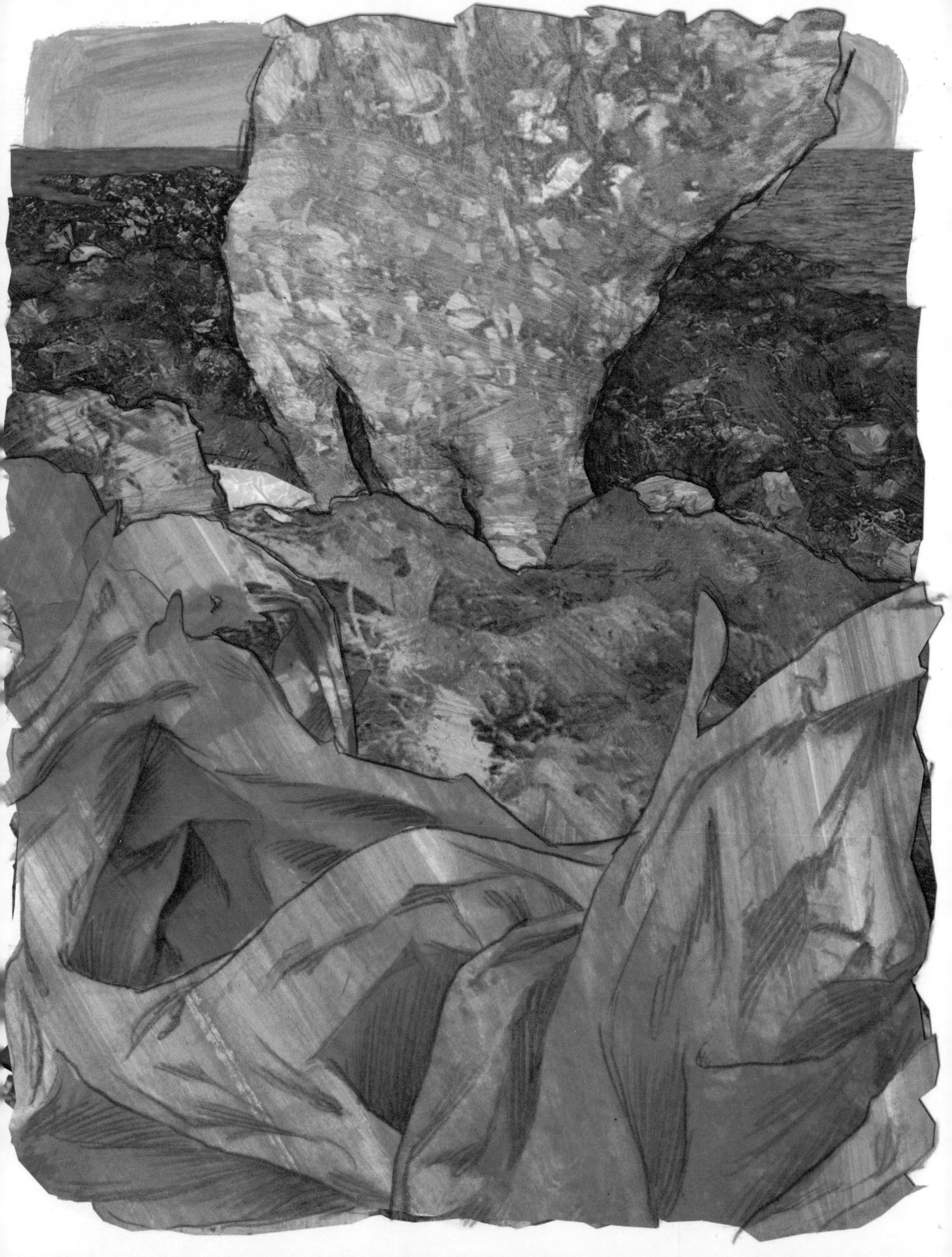

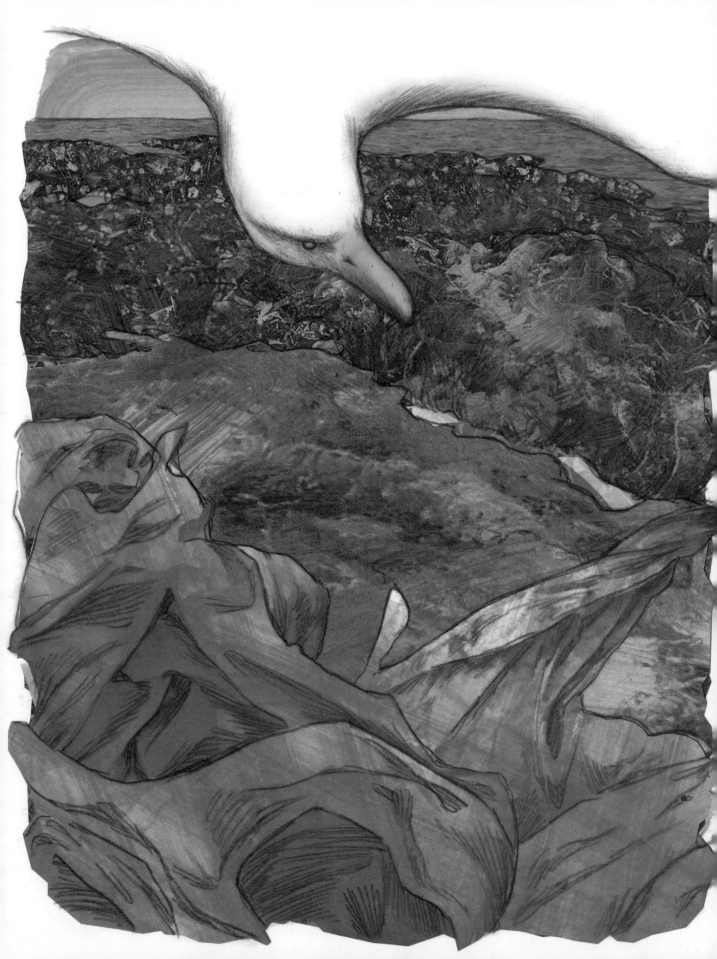

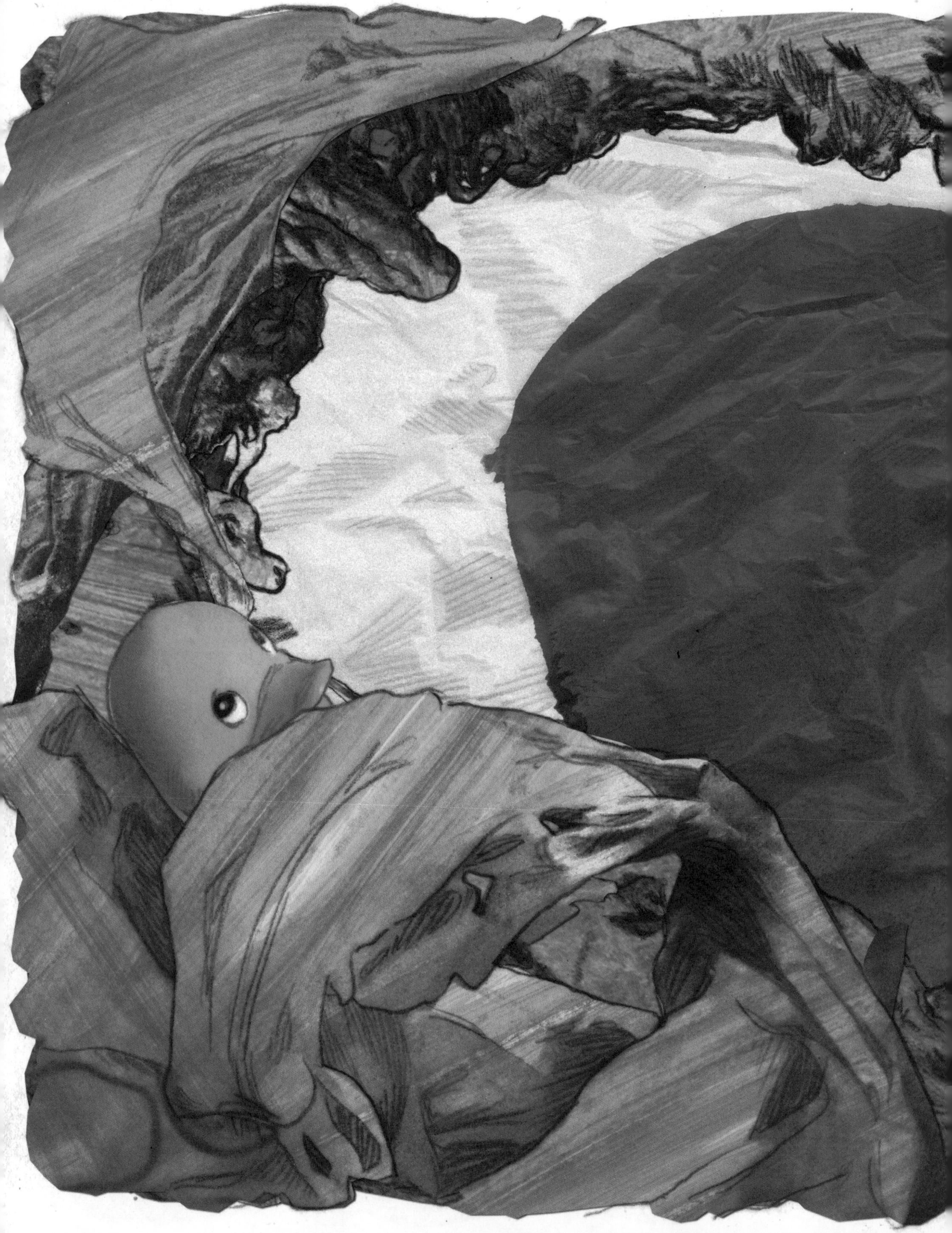

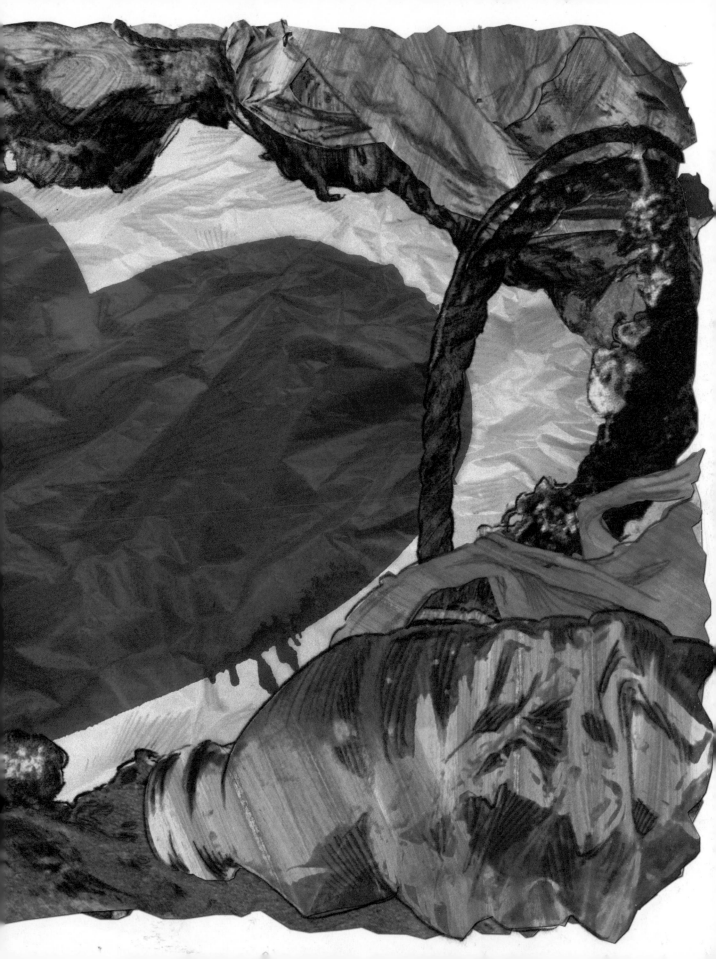

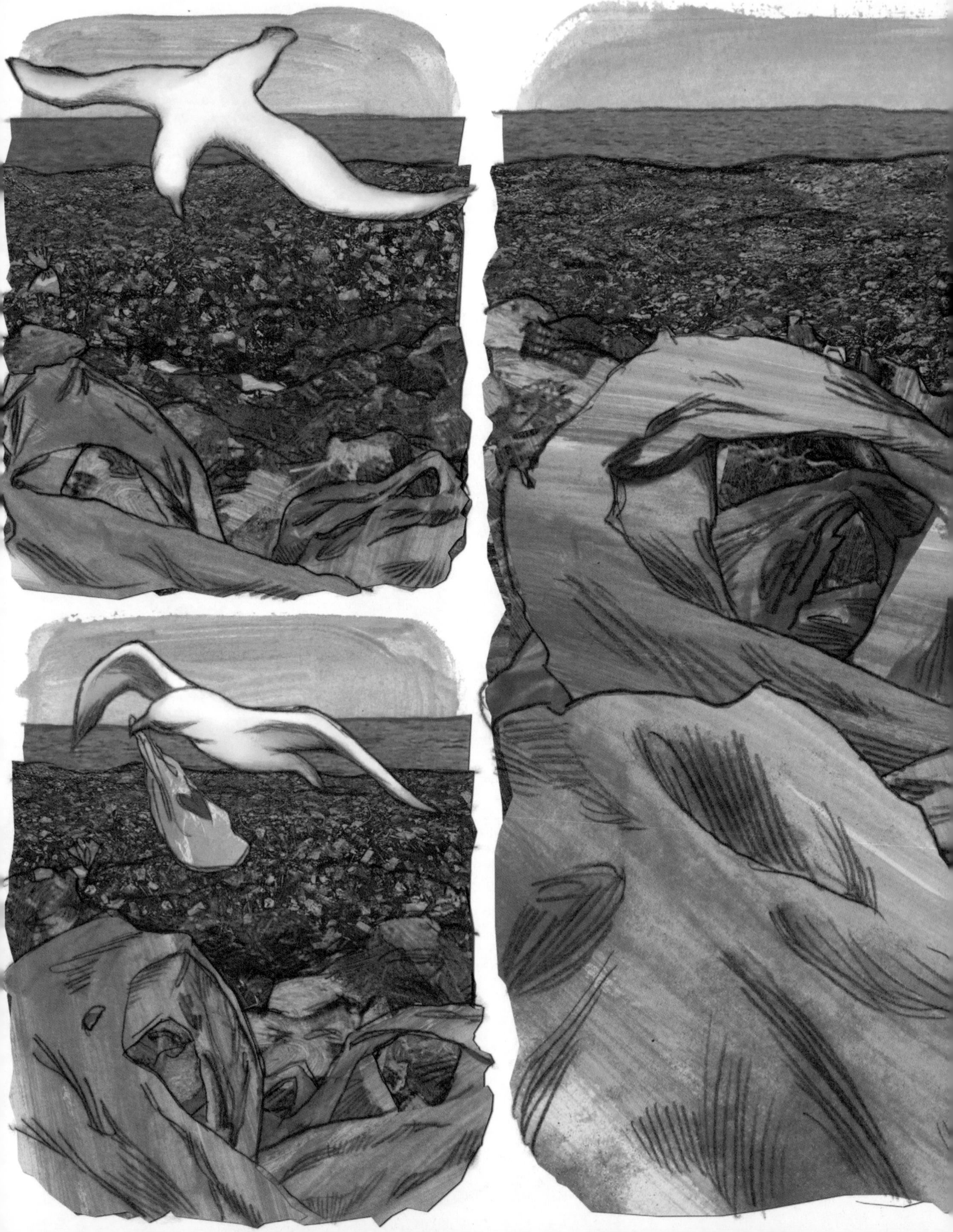

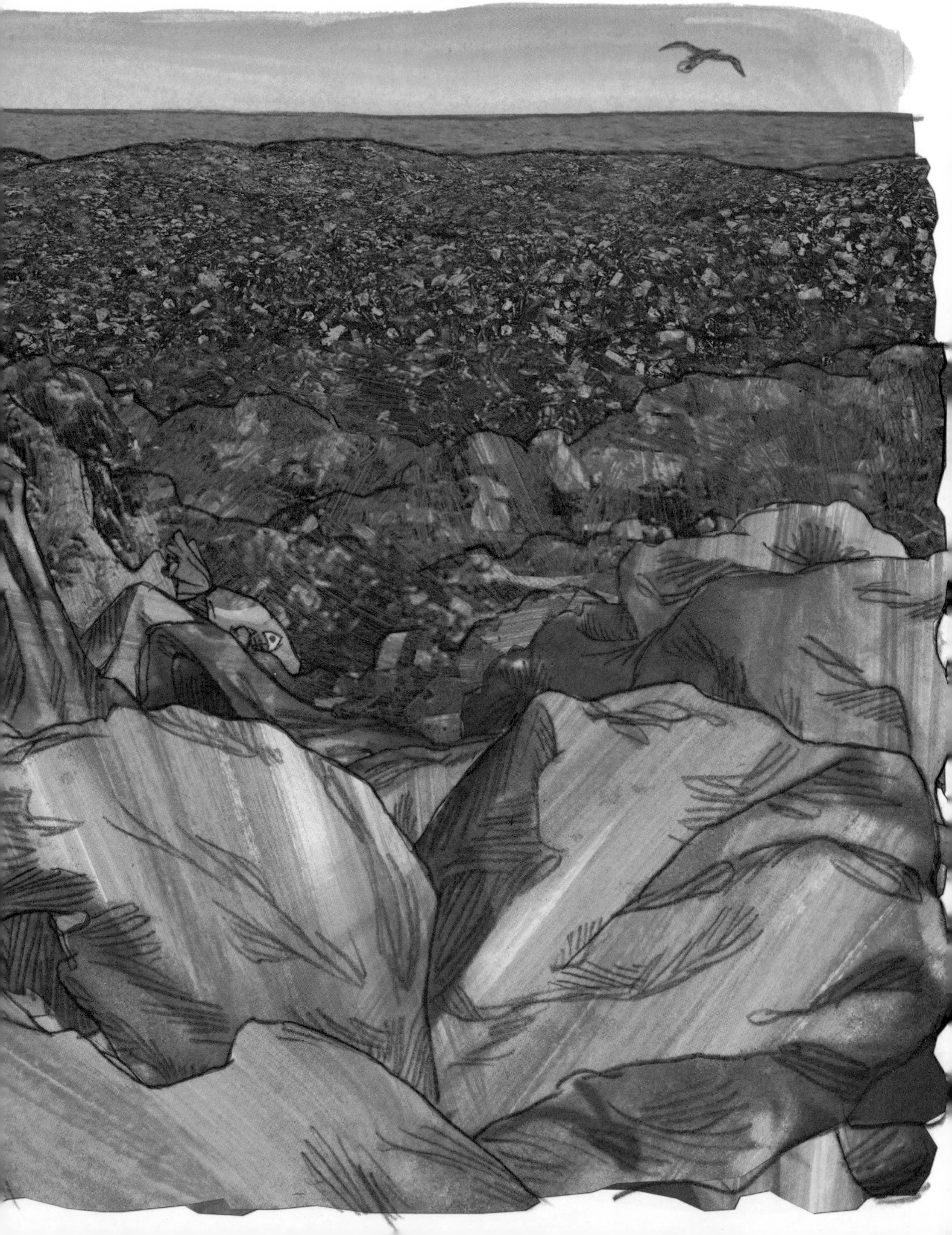

# five

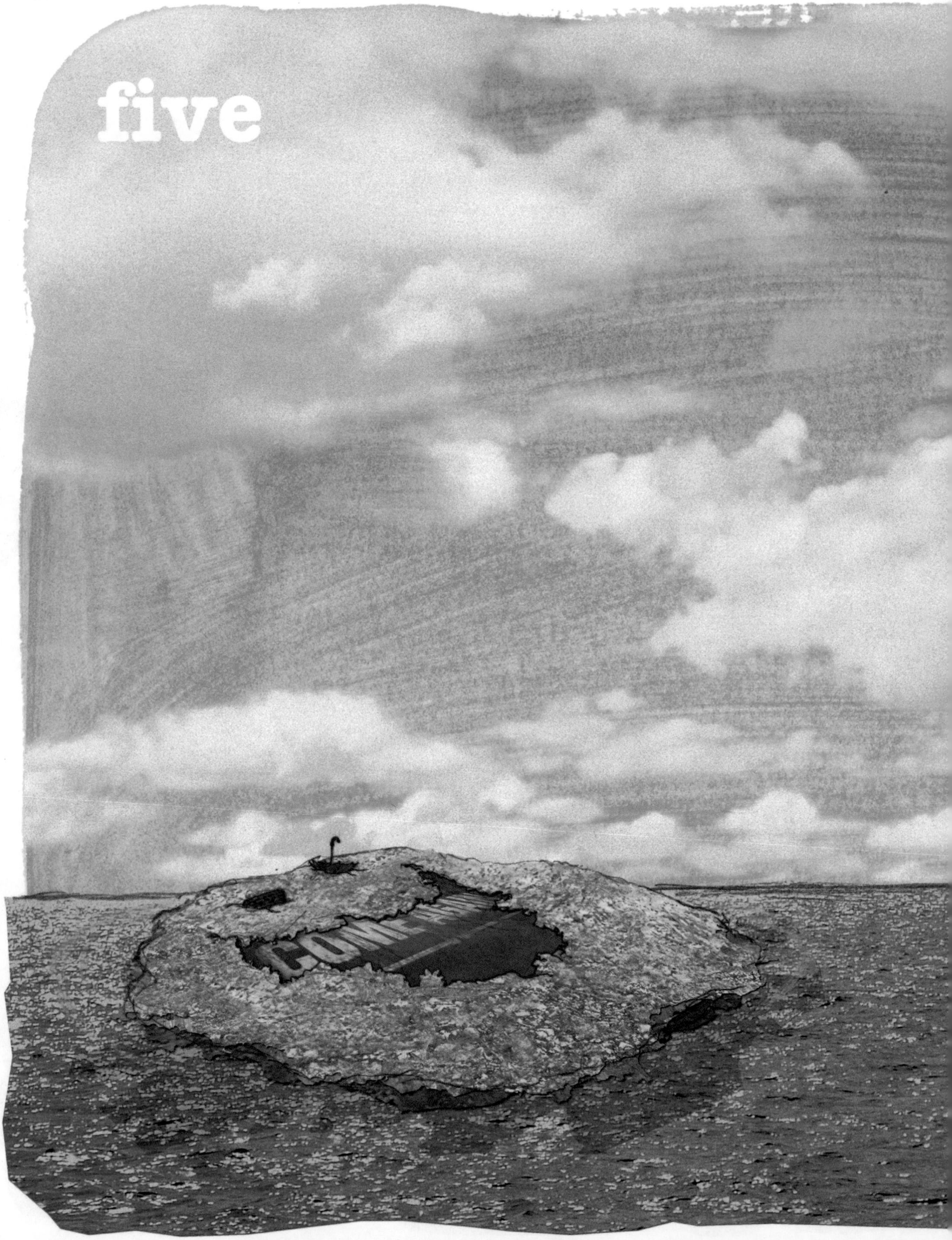
COME

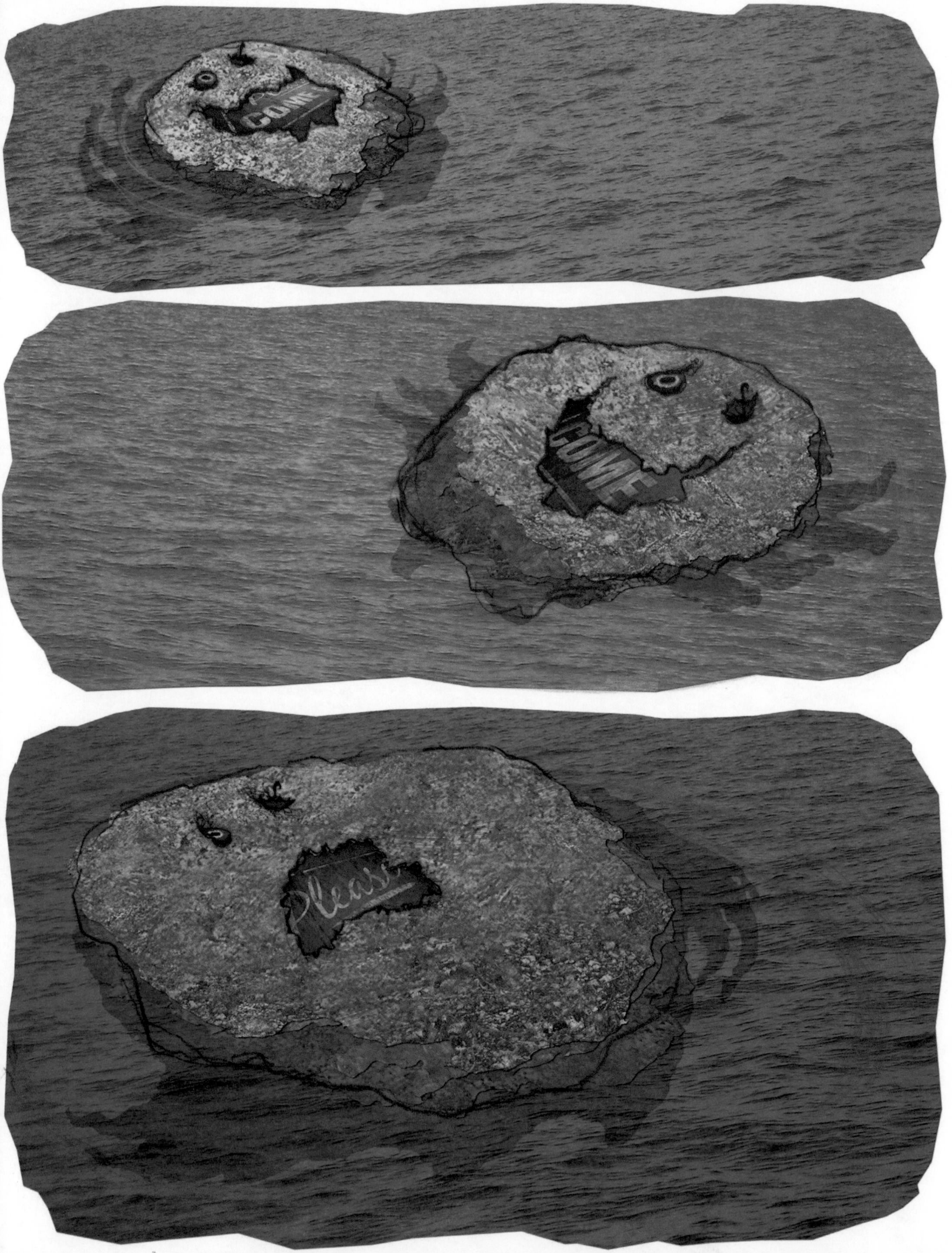
COME
COME
Pleas

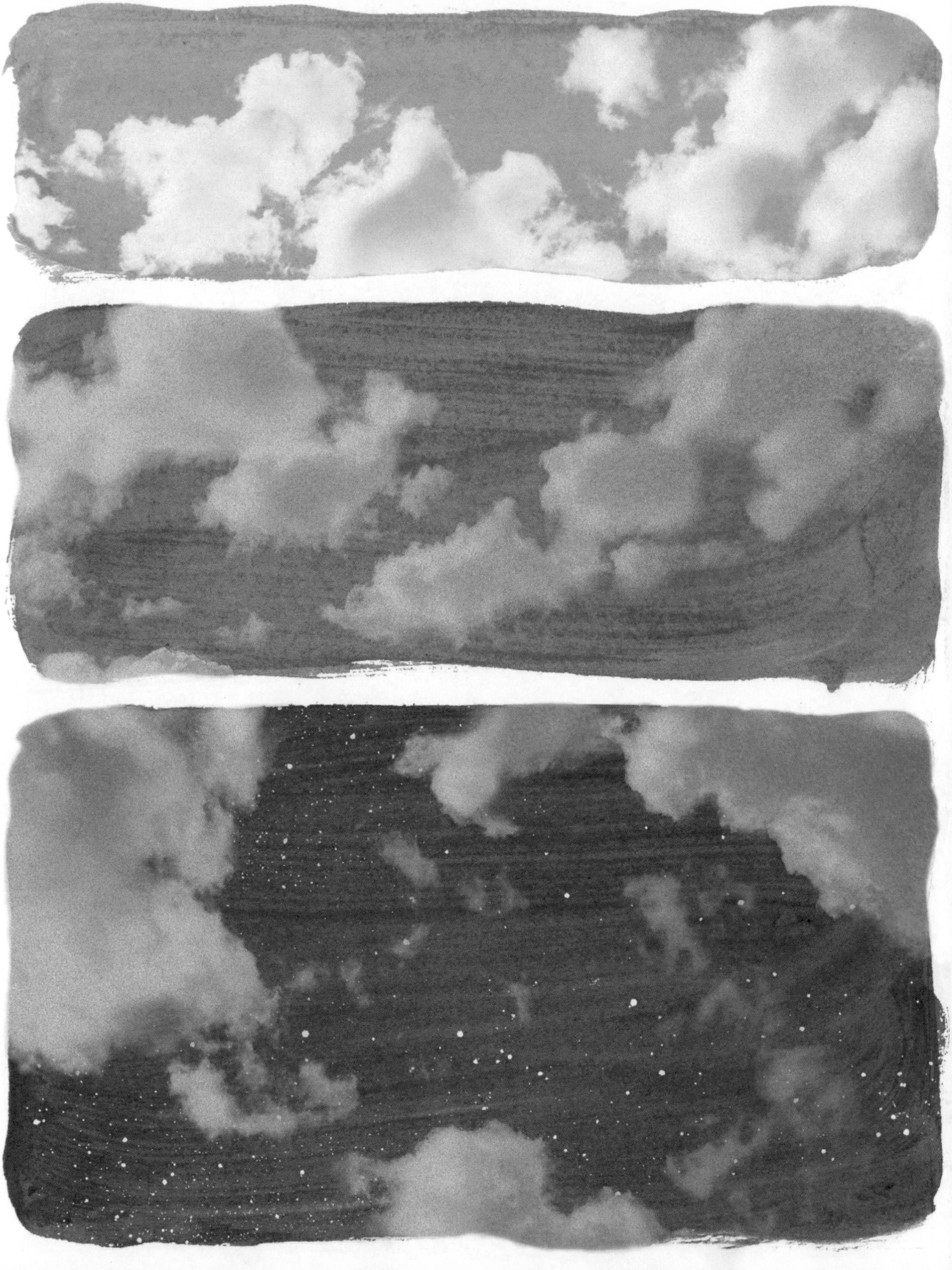

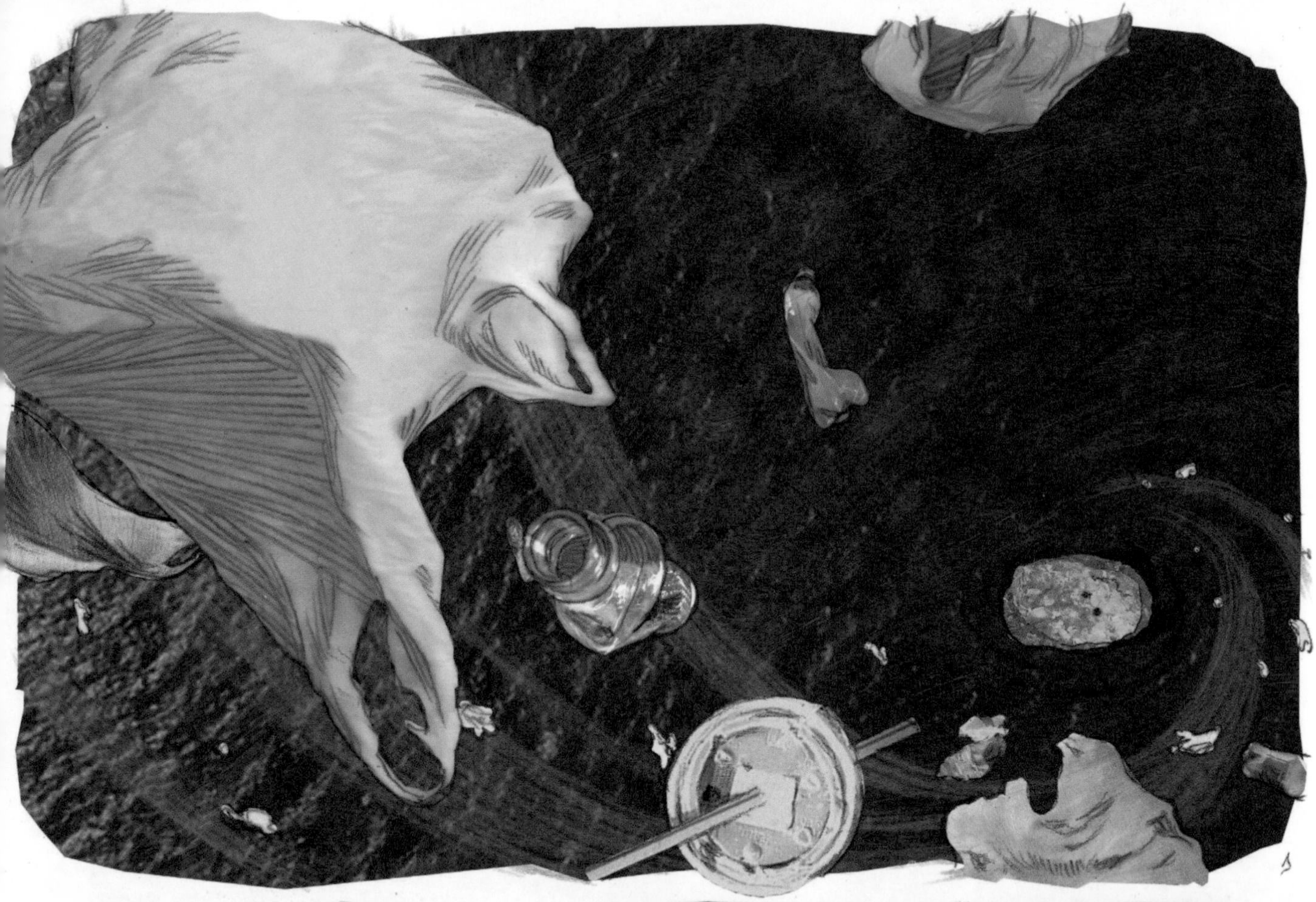

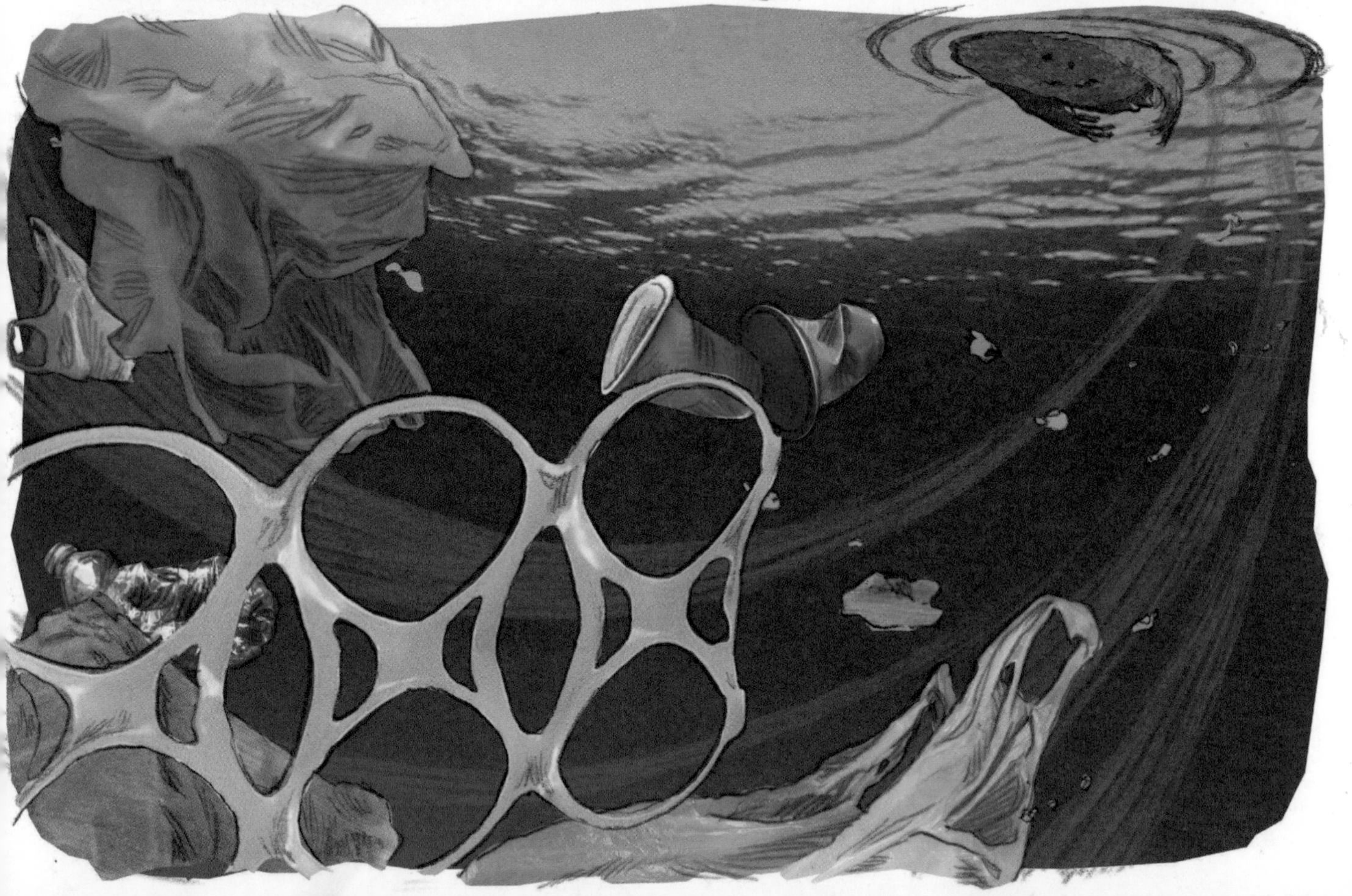

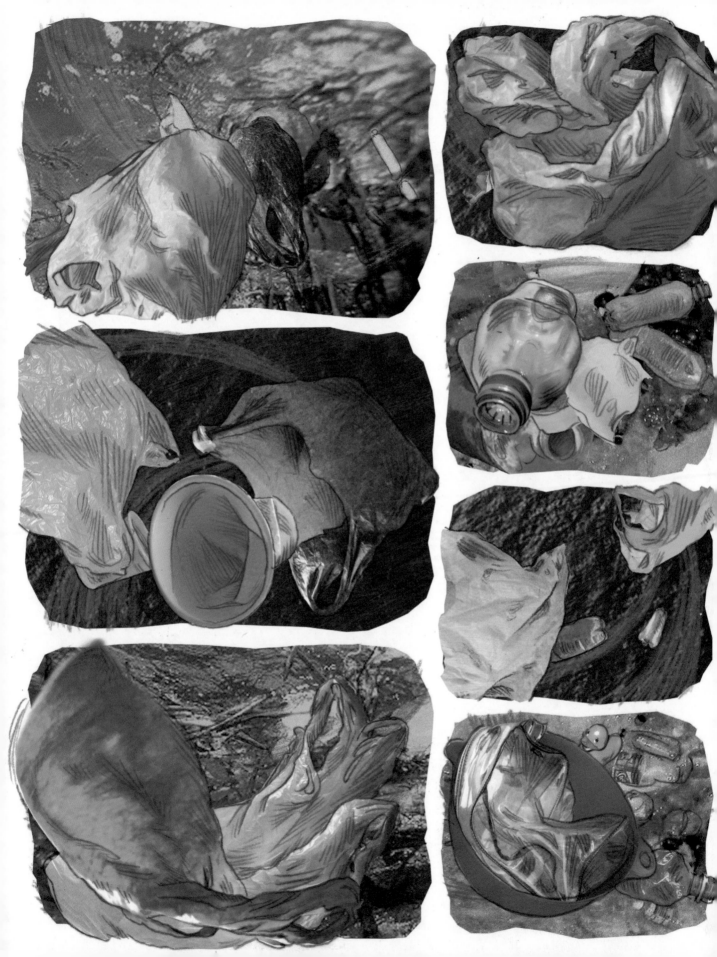

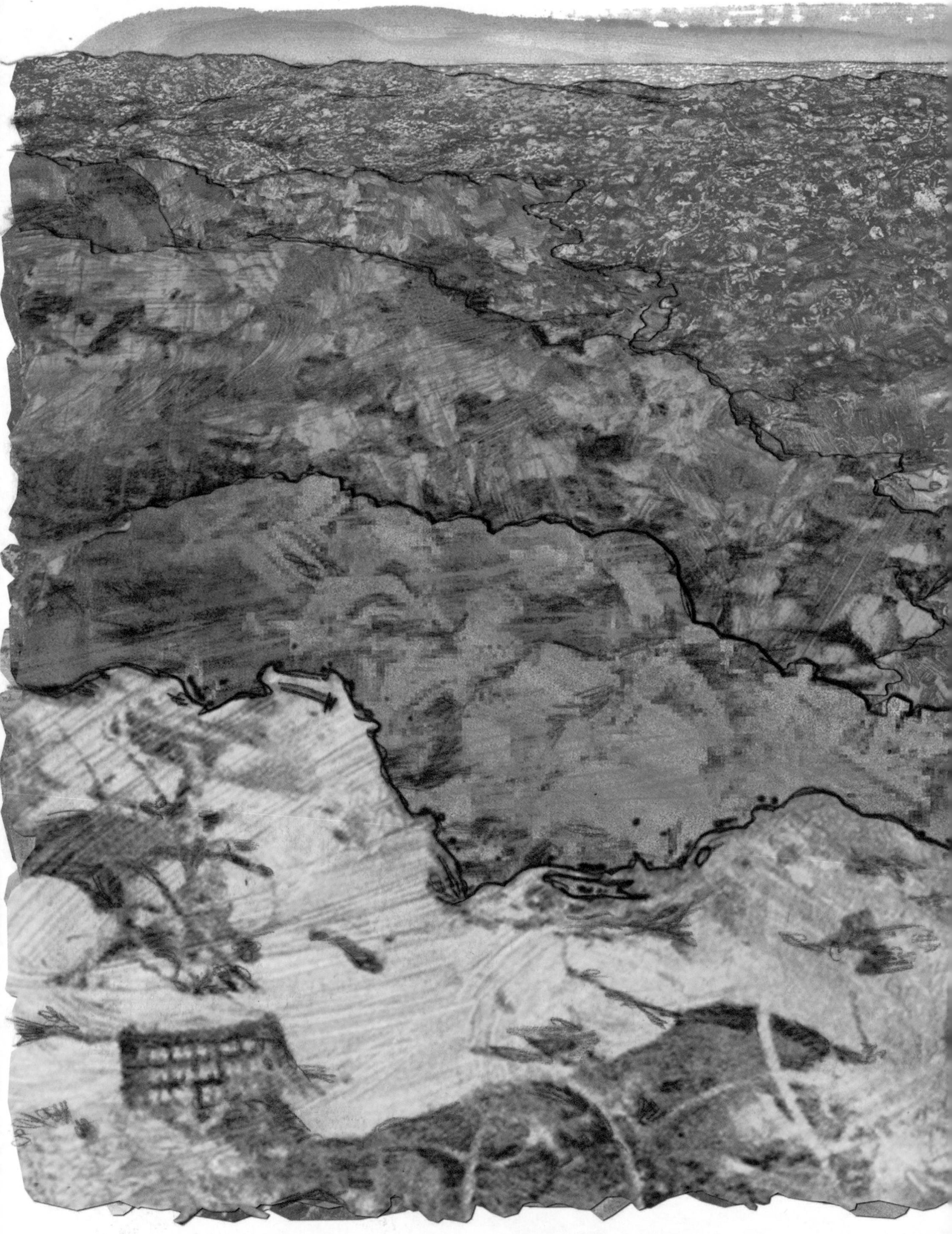

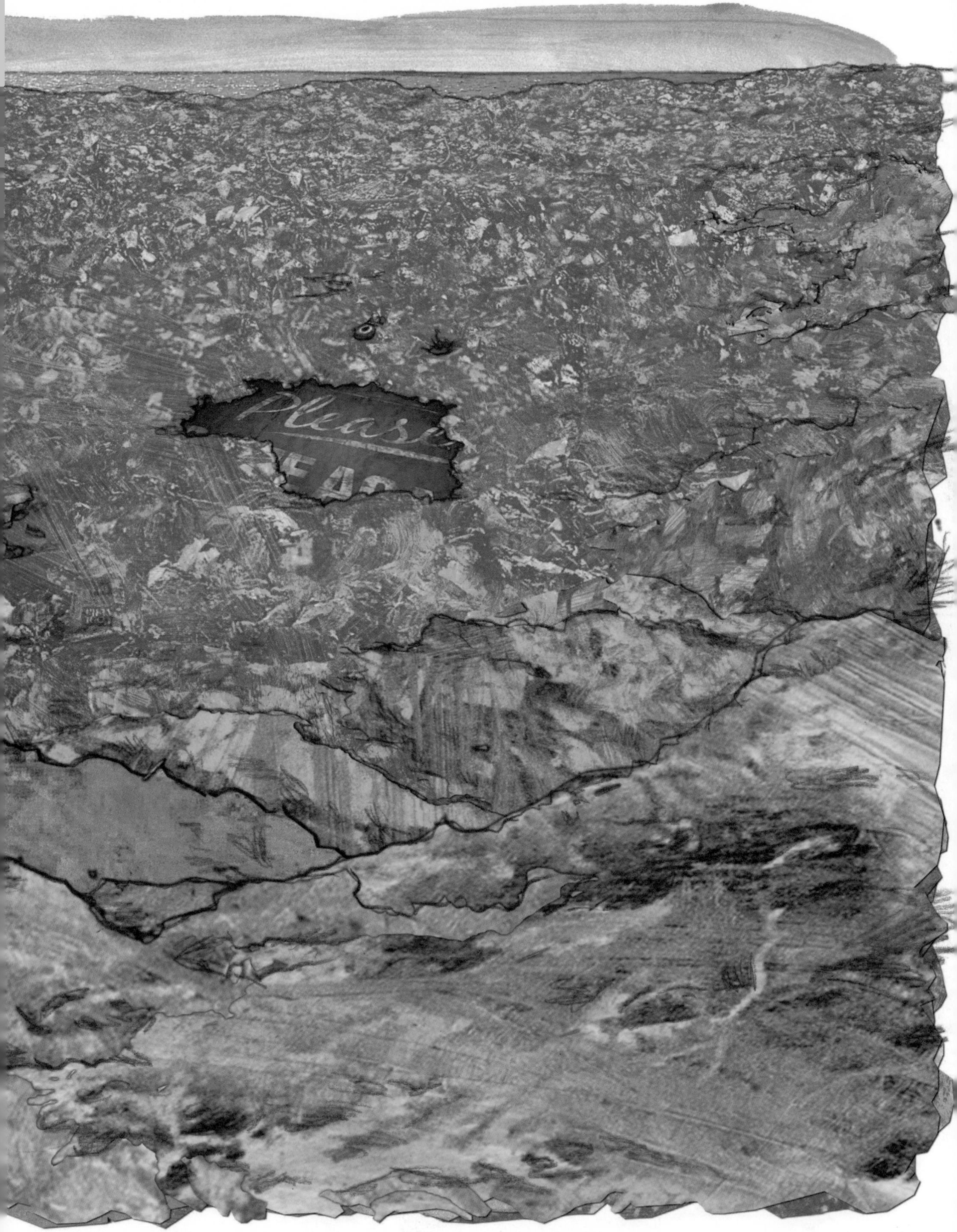
Please

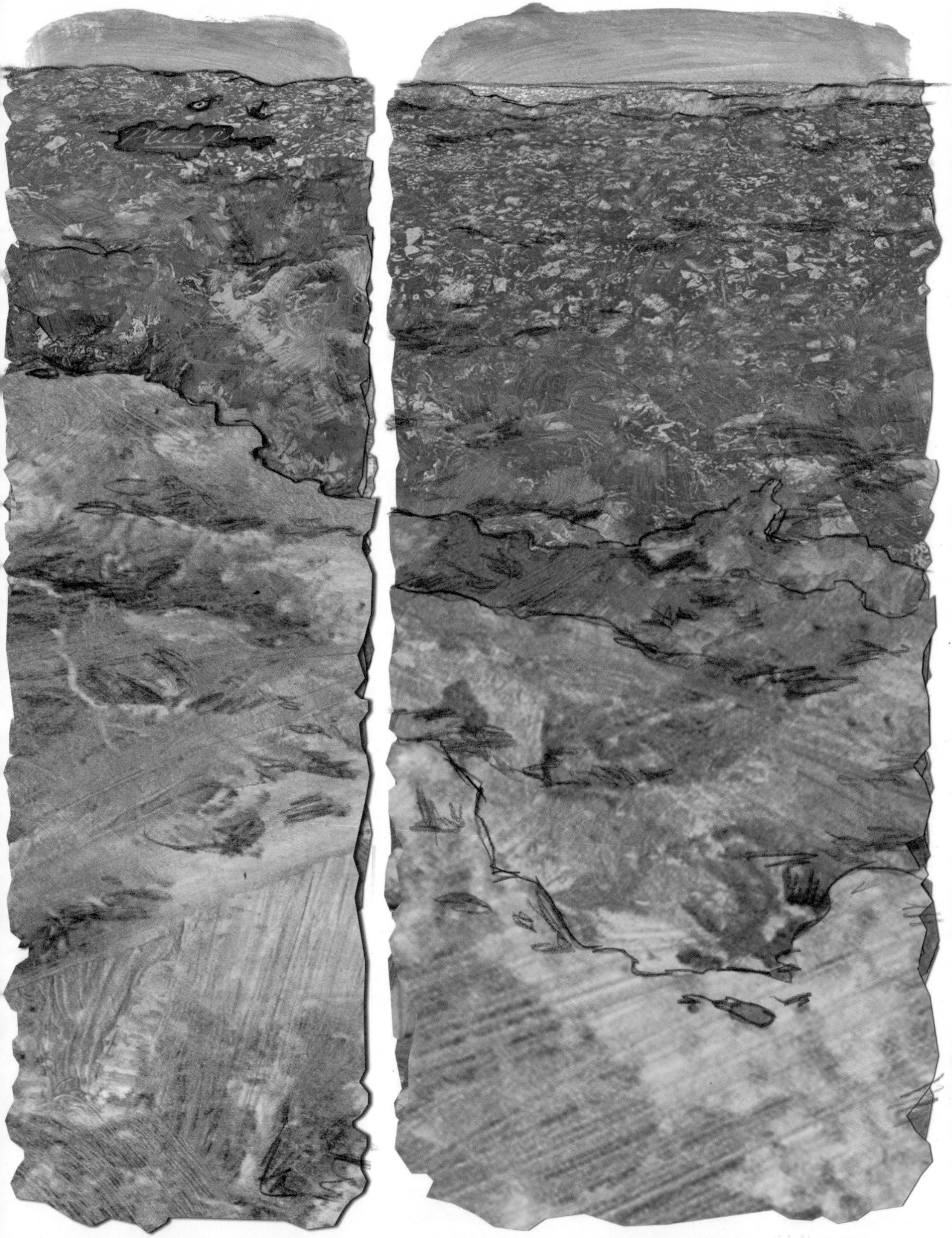
Please

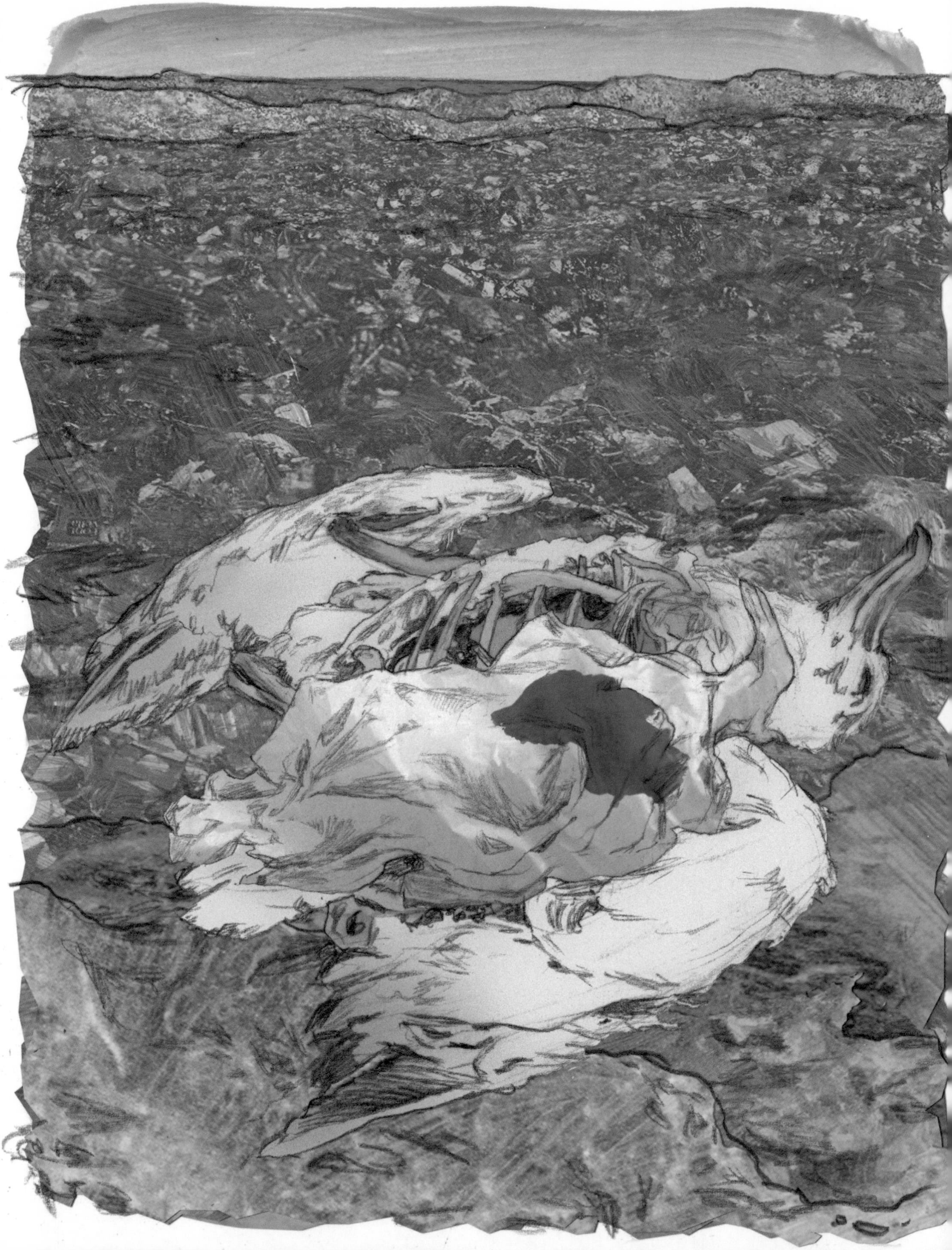

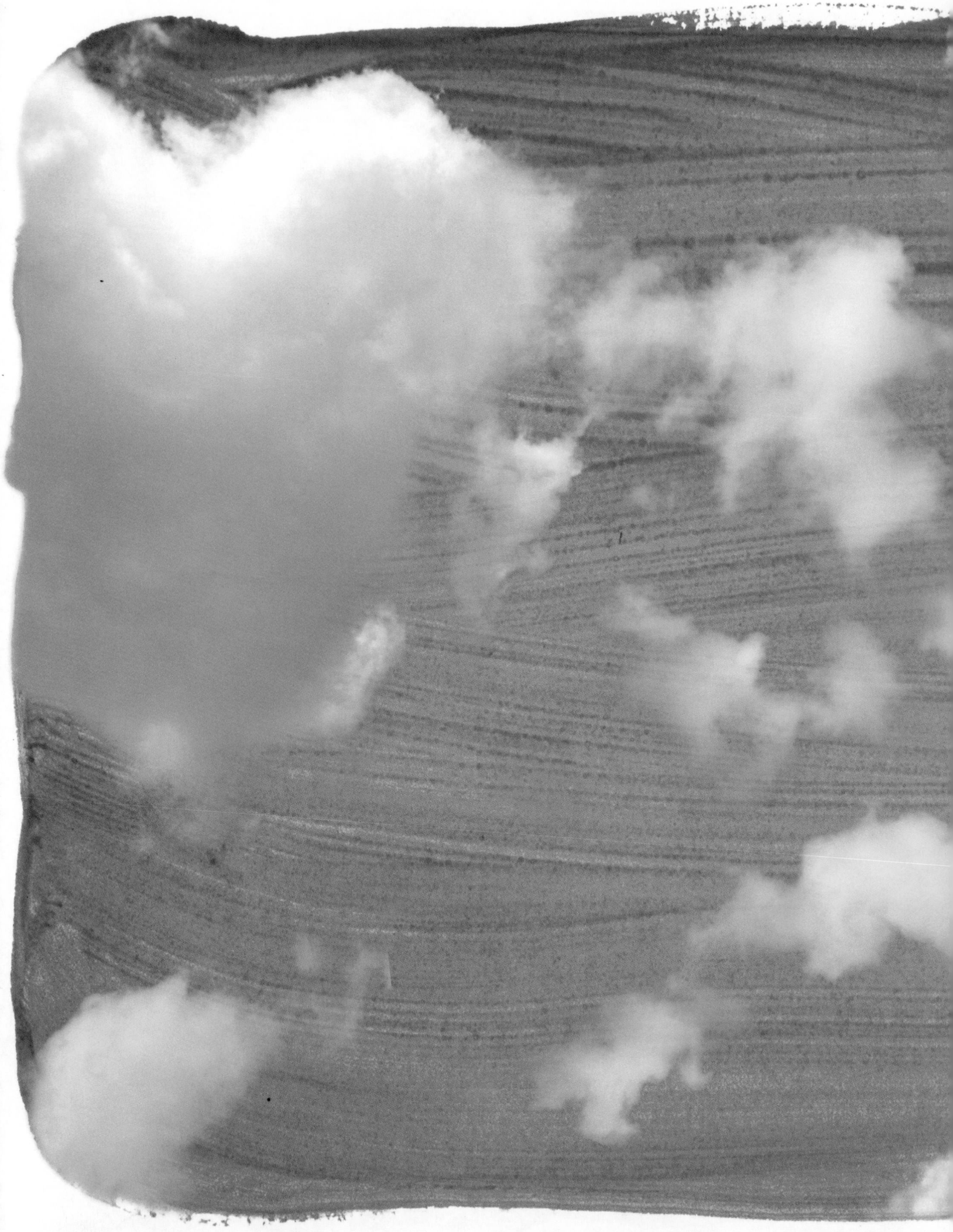

# six

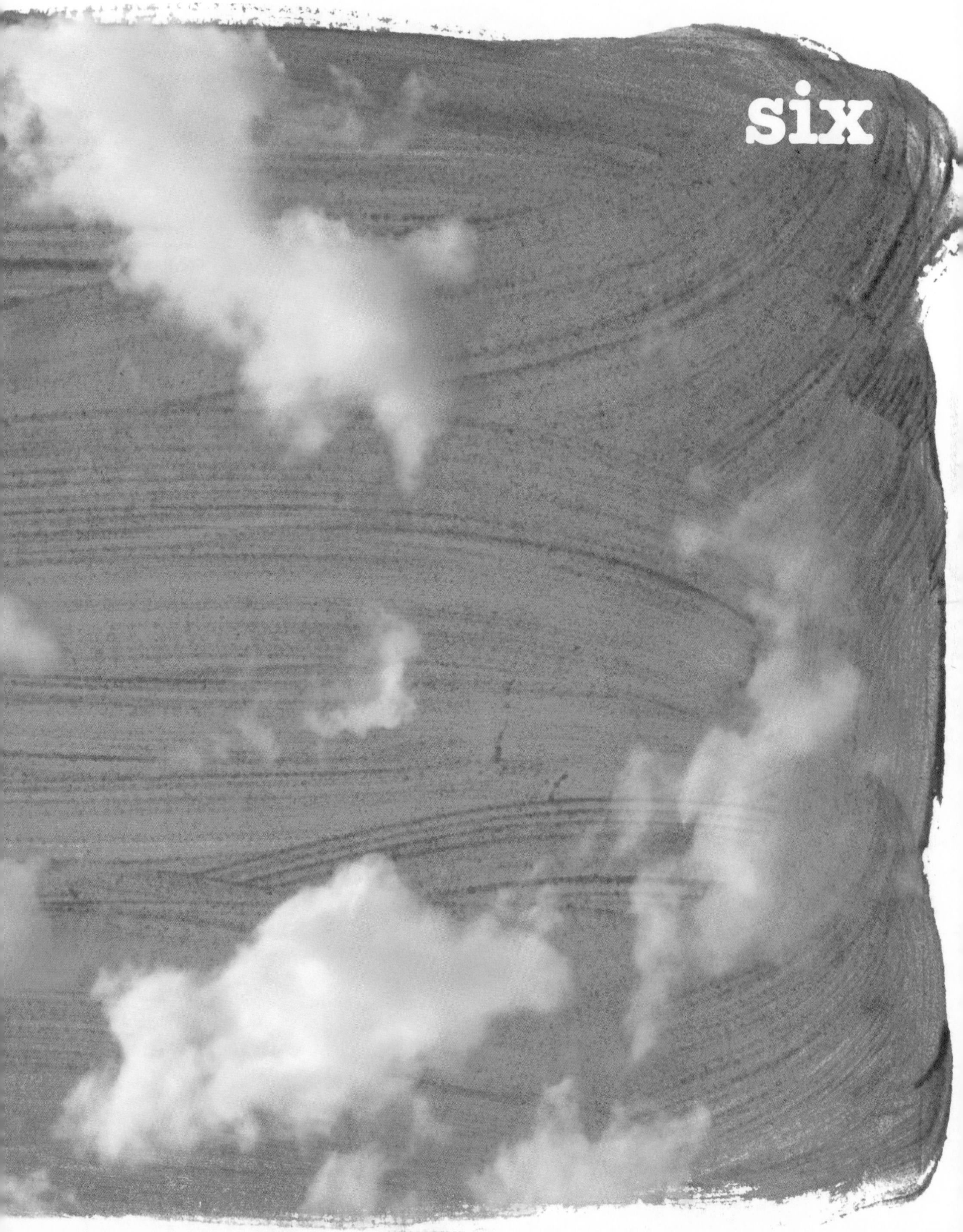

HELLO

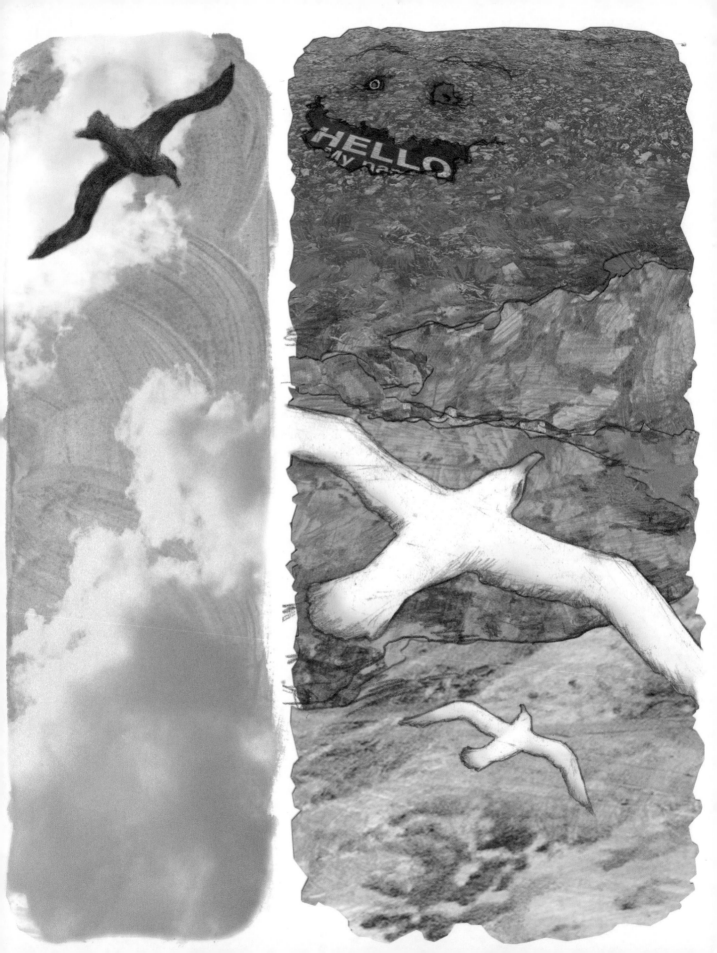

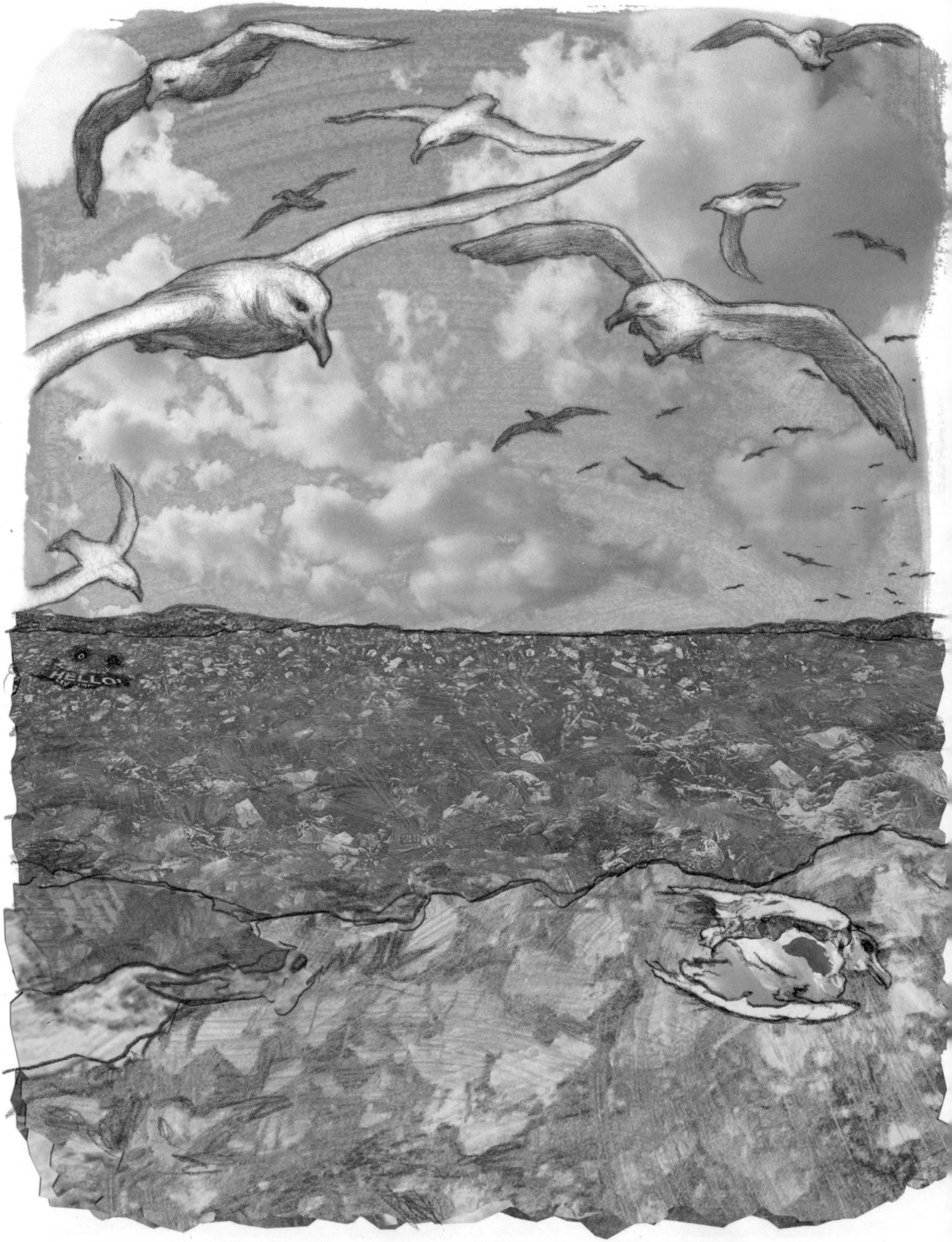
HELLO!

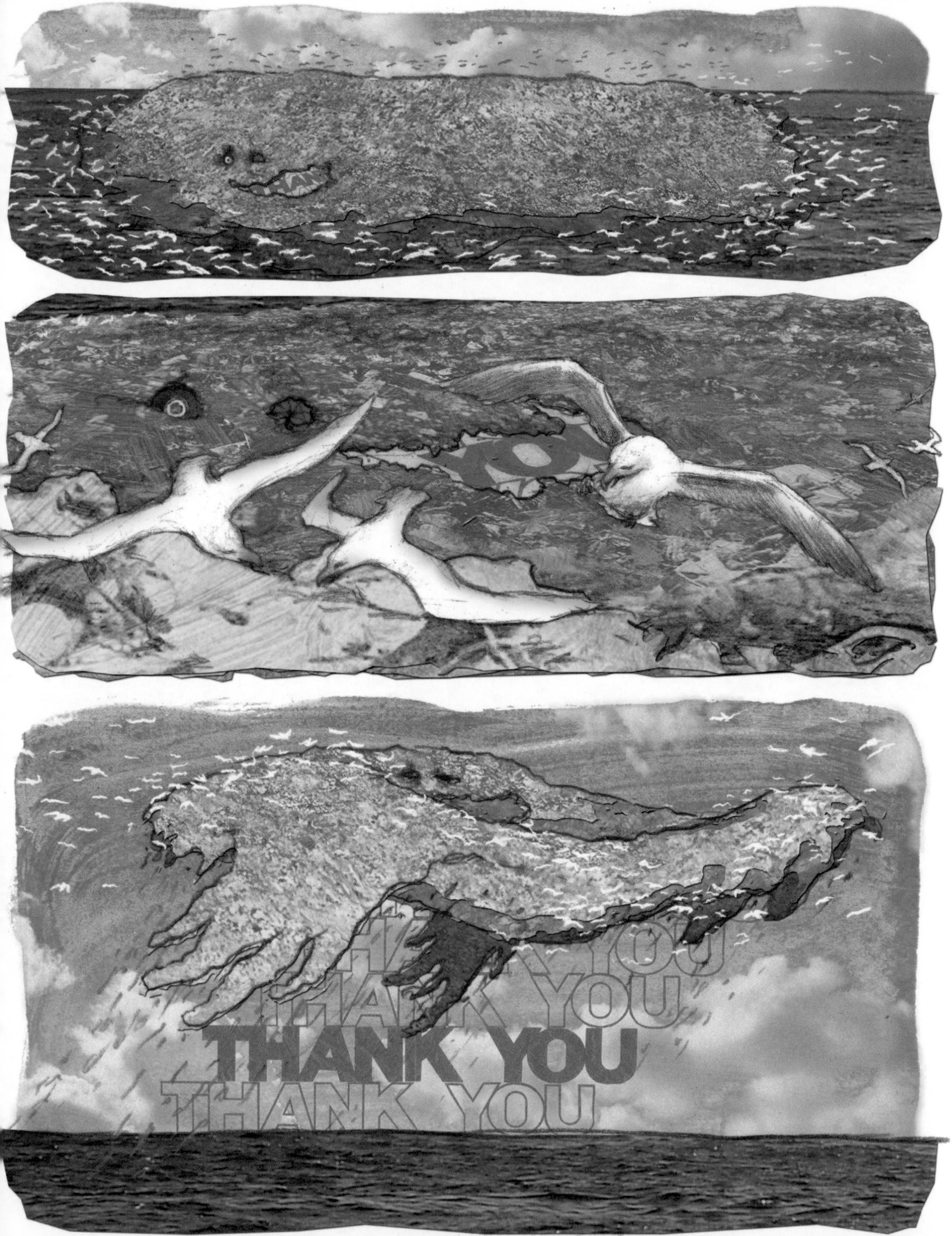
THANK YOU
THANK YOU

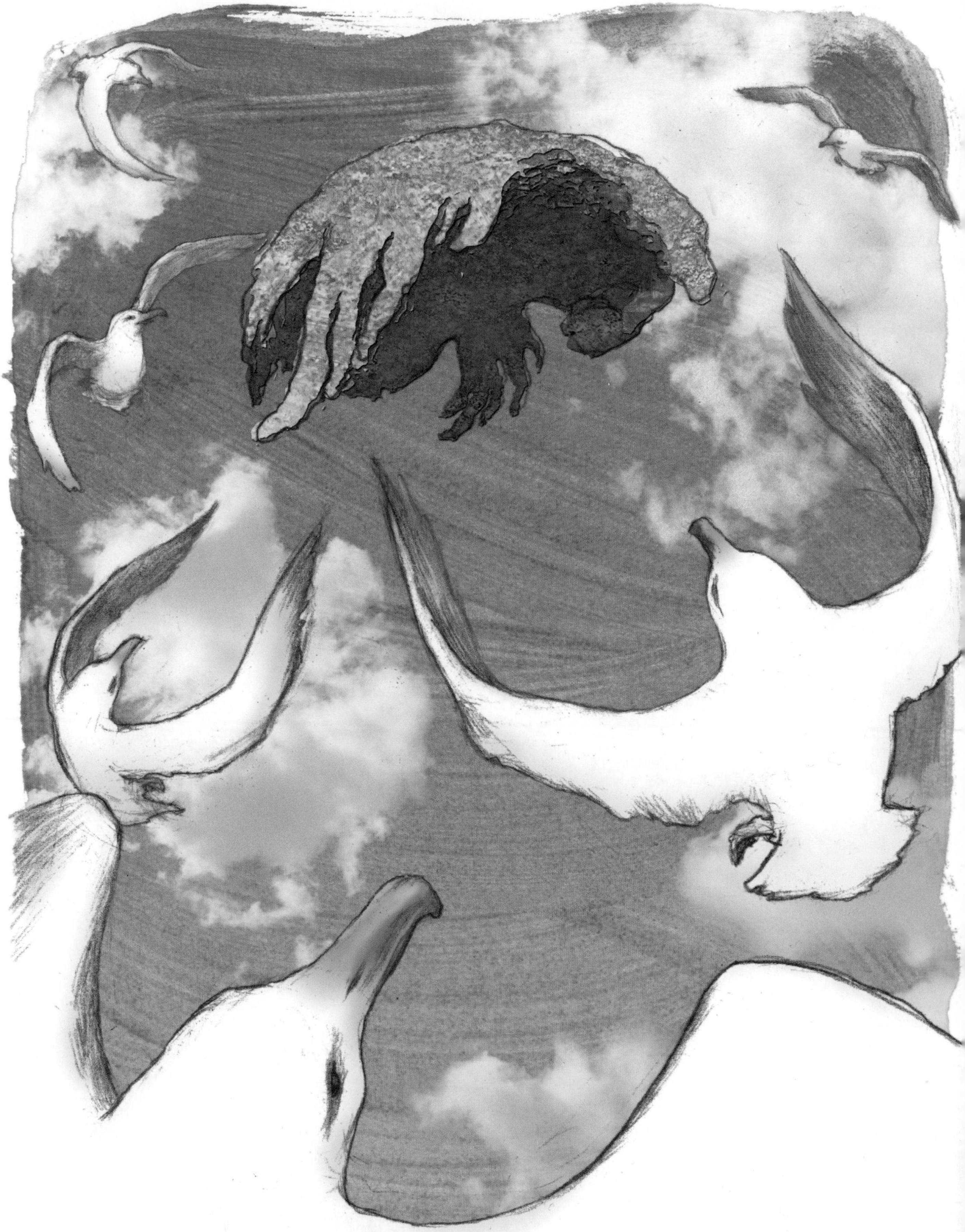

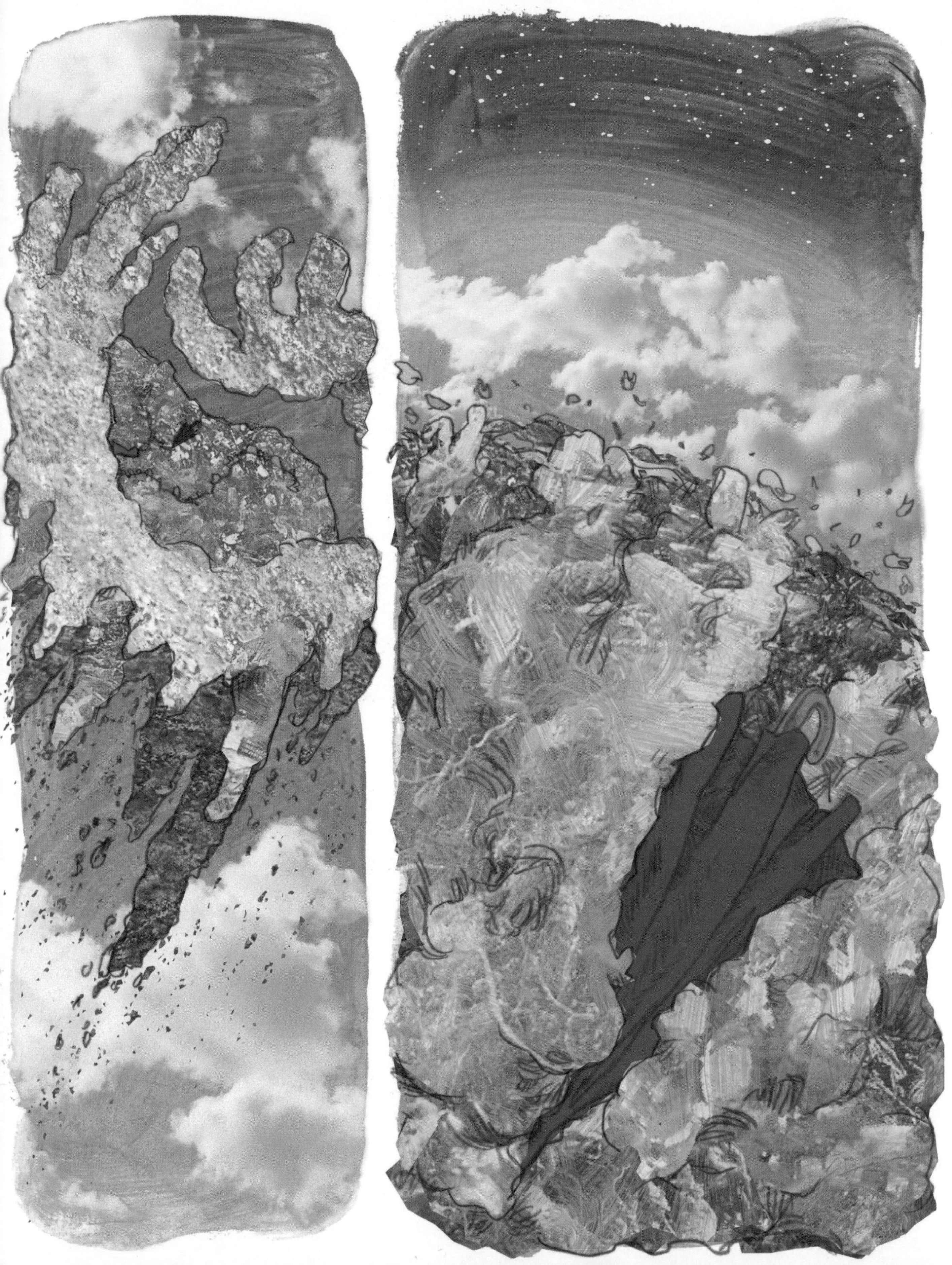

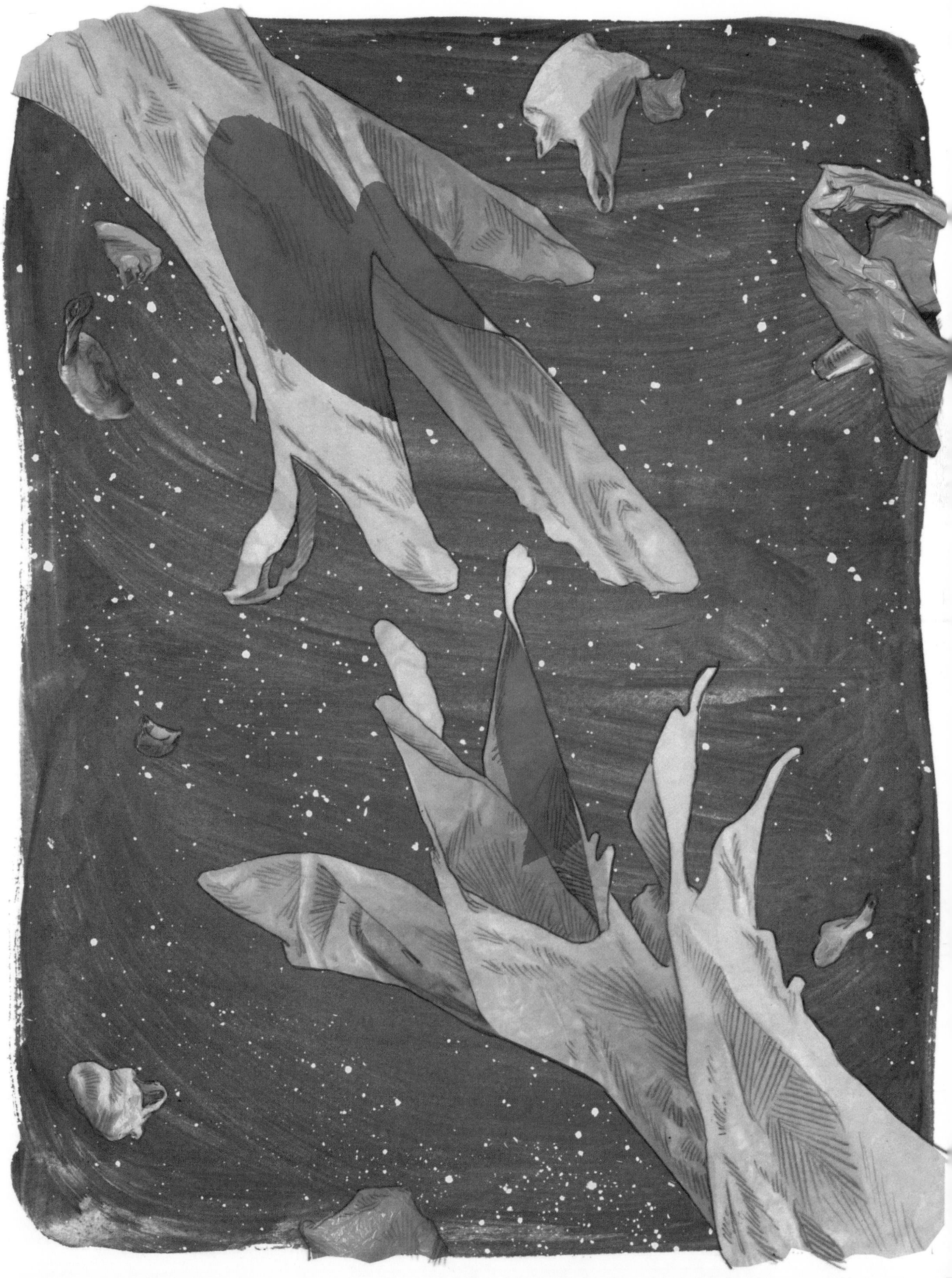

# epilogue

end

JEFF CORWIN CONNECT™ presents

# I'm not an ocean polluter

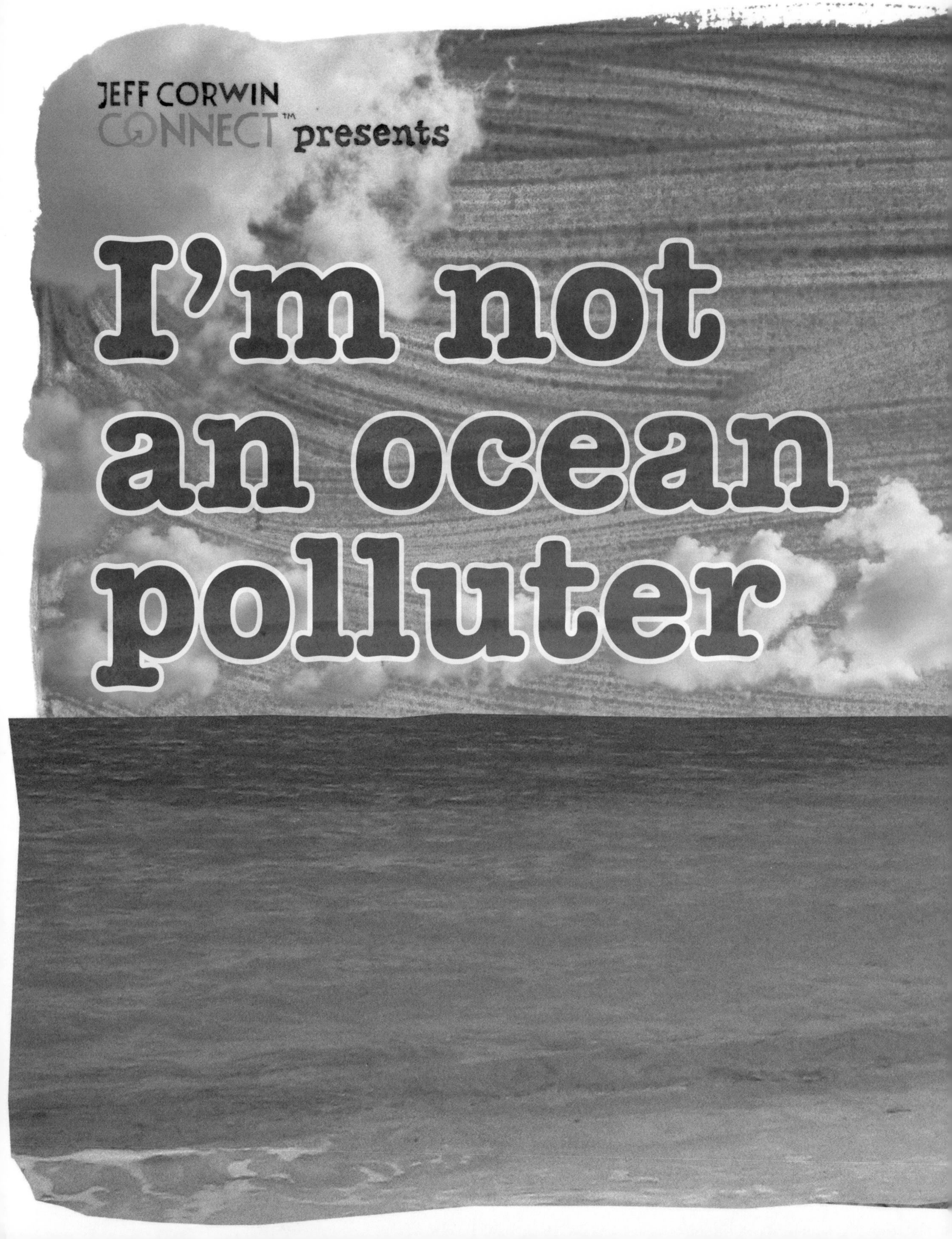

Information about the human impact on our oceans and ways you can get involved in the movement to save our seas!

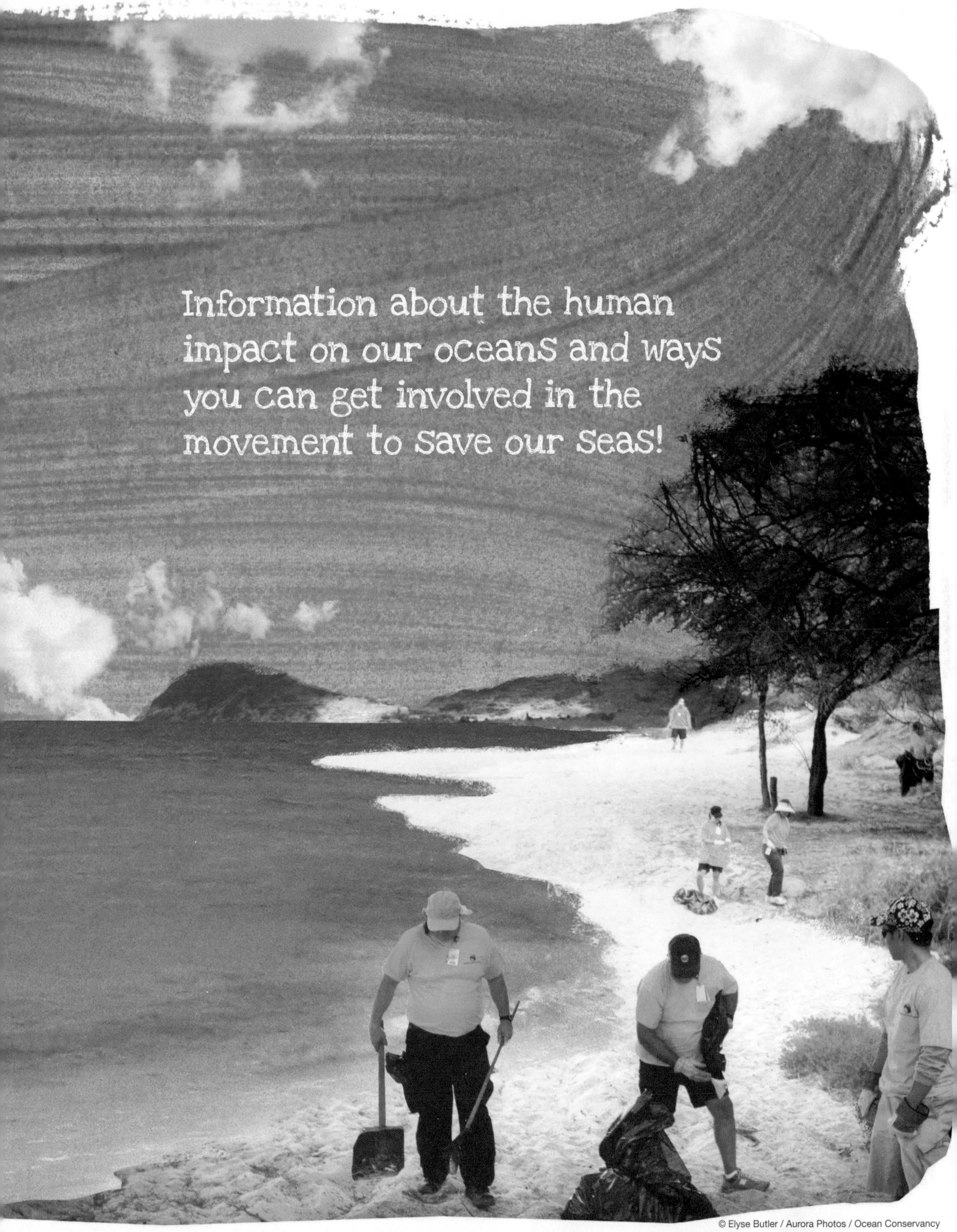

© Elyse Butler / Aurora Photos / Ocean Conservancy

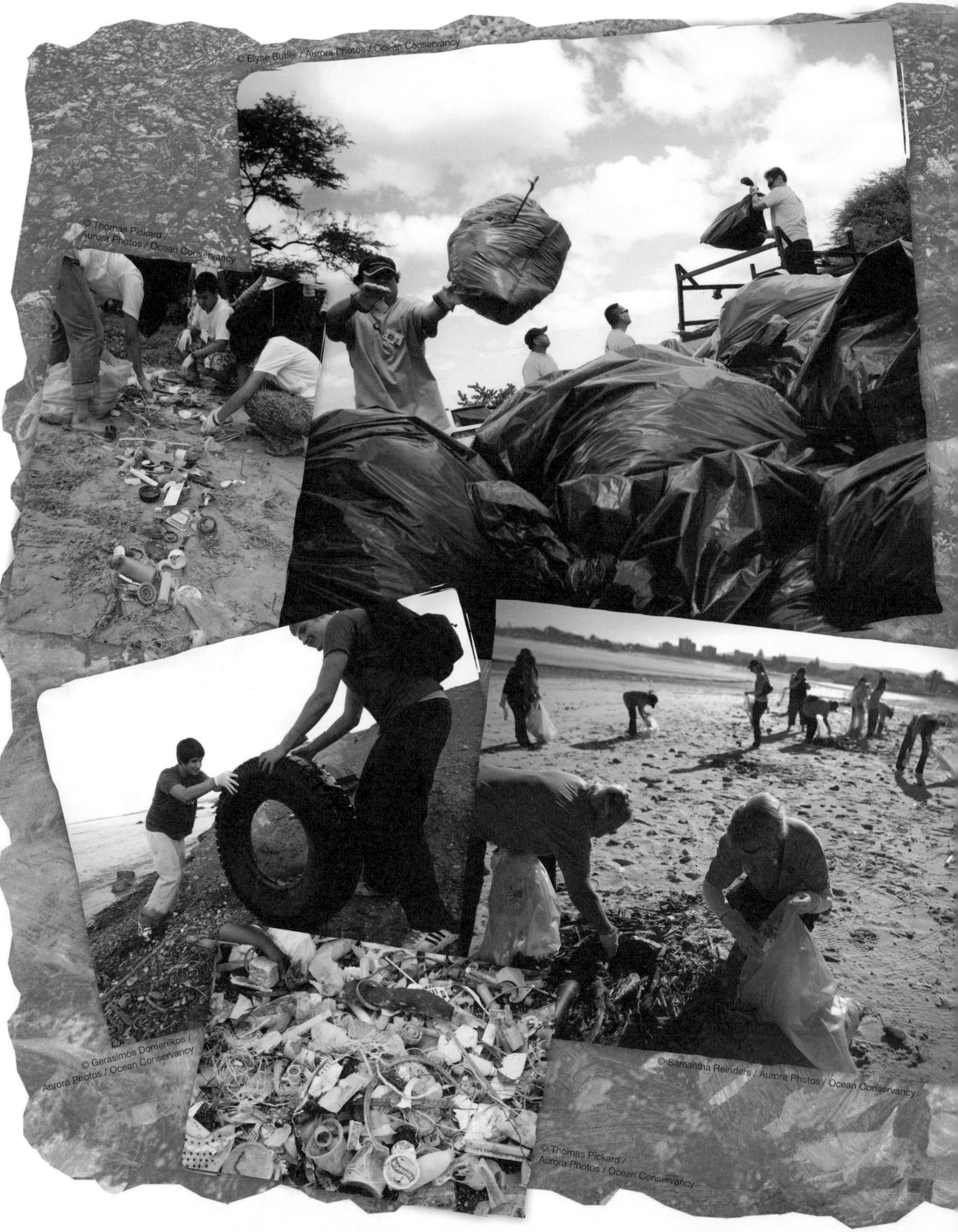

© Elyse Butler / Aurora Photos / Ocean Conservancy

© Thomas Pickard / Aurora Photos / Ocean Conservancy

© Gerasimos Domenikos / Aurora Photos / Ocean Conservancy

© Samantha Reinders / Aurora Photos / Ocean Conservancy

© Thomas Pickard / Aurora Photos / Ocean Conservancy

# The North Pacific Gyre

## or

## The Great Pacific Garbage Patch

Rachel Hope Allison's *I'm Not a Plastic Bag* is an artistic reimagining of a very real phenomenon. The North Pacific Subtropical Gyre, more commonly referred to as the Great Pacific Garbage Patch, is an accumulated concentration of floating trash between Hawaii and the California coastline. Cyclical ocean wind and current patterns create a vortex for ocean debris, most of which is human consumer waste, such as plastic bags and bottles. A number of these gyres exist in the world, highlighting the incredibly damaging effect human consumer waste has on our ocean.

The Garbage Patch does not appear as a giant floating landfill, however, but rather a trash stew or an "archipelago of trash." While there are areas of dense debris, much more common are seemingly barren swatches of ocean full of broken down debris called *nurdles*, or *micro plastics* when the particles are even too small to see. These particles float submerged in the top few meters of calm seas and create their own hazards to marine life. Much of the larger debris in the oceans also remains submerged, making data collection on the Gyre an extremely complex and difficult task for scientists.

The Pacific Garbage Patch was first publicized by Charles Moore of the Algalita Marine Research Foundation in 1997.[1] Since then, the Patch has sparked the interest of both the public and the scientific community. Nicholas Mallos, a marine scientist and team member of Ocean Conservancy's Trash Free Seas® Program,[2] traveled to the North Pacific Gyre with Project Kaisei,[3] a cleanup initiative of the Ocean Voyages Institute.[4] In just one day alone, Mallos collected 4,000 pieces of plastic, 27 rope fragments, 11 fishing nets, and an assortment of disposable consumer plastics.[5]

"The ocean is an expansive, awe-inspiring body of water, and there's something new to discover every day," says Mallos. "At the same time, its size and complexity make it that much harder to find definitive answers. While we do know that ocean pollution poses threats to animals and humans, there's still a lot we don't know.

"The good news? Anyone and everyone can be a part of the solution for Trash Free Seas®. As a consumer, you can stop trash at its source. Make choices like recycling, drinking from reusable bottles and eliminating one-time use items like bags, bottles and straws."[6]

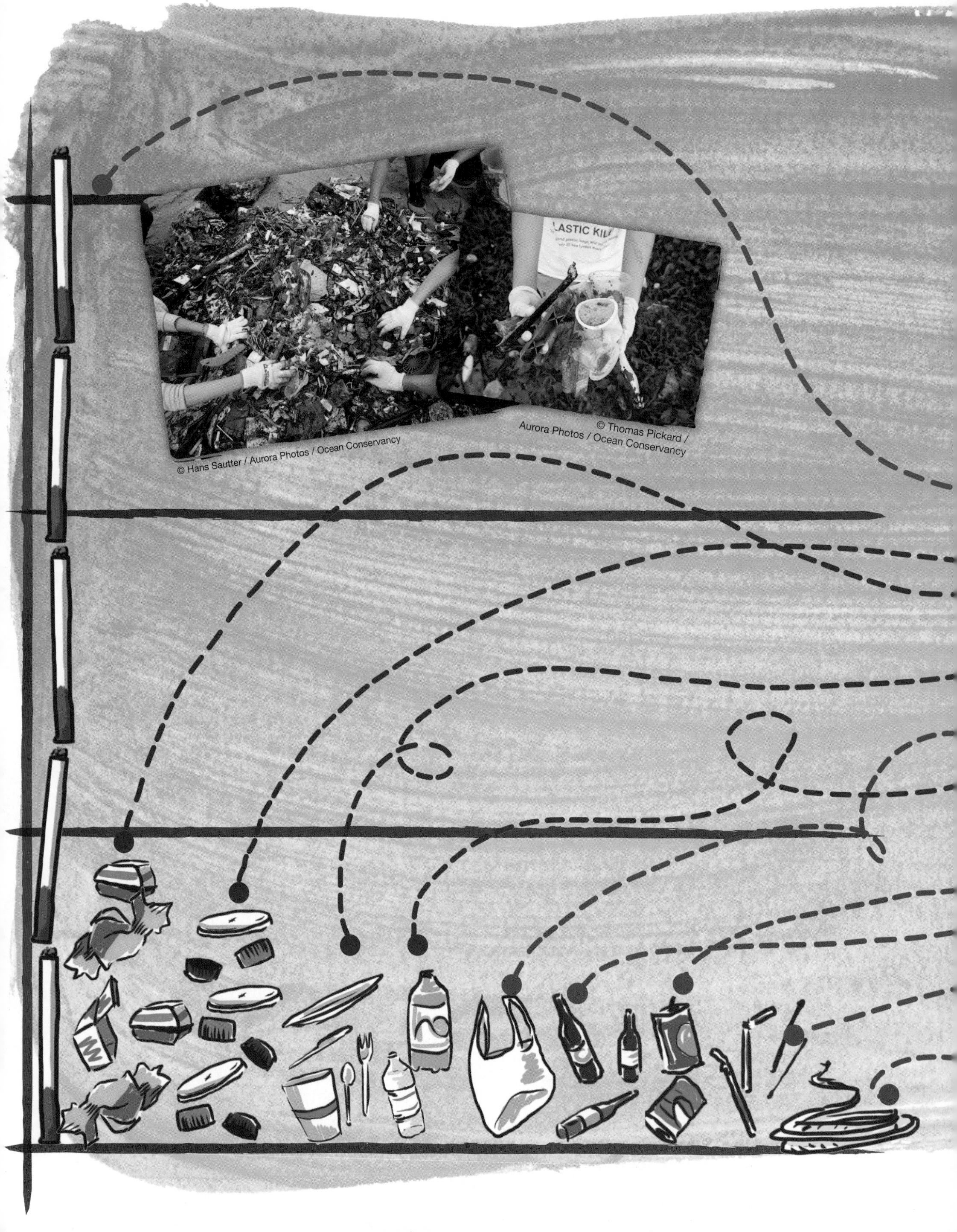
© Hans Sautter / Aurora Photos / Ocean Conservancy

© Thomas Pickard / Aurora Photos / Ocean Conservancy

# TOP TEN Items Found in Ocean Debris*

1. Cigarettes ............................................................ 32%
2. Food Wrappers/Containers ....................... 9%
3. Caps, Lids ......................................................... 8%
4. Cups, Plates, Forks, Knives, Spoons ...... 6%
5. Beverage Bottles (Plastic) .......................... 6%
6. Bags (Plastic) .................................................. 5%
7. Beverage Bottles (Glass) ............................ 4%
8. Beverage Cans ............................................... 4%
9. Straws/Stirrers .............................................. 4%
10. Rope .................................................................... 2%

*Logged by International Coastal Cleanup® volunteers over a 25-year period.

*Information for this chart provided by Ocean Conservancy/International Coastal Cleanup®.[1]

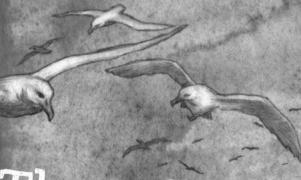

# Threatened Marine Wildlife

## Loggerhead Sea Turtle

While loggerhead sea turtles are one of the more prevalent marine turtle species, they have been classified as threatened by the US Fish and Wildlife Service since 1978.[1] Many factors contribute to their dwindling numbers, including ocean pollution. Loggerheads often mistake plastic bags and other debris for food sources like jellyfish, whelks, and conchs.[23] Ocean debris on beaches also threatens nesting females, as well as hatchlings trying to make their way to the surf.[4]

## Hawaiian Monk Seal

Preferring warmer climates than their Arctic brothers, the Hawaiian Monk Seal lives only in the Northern Hawaiian Islands. Its numbers have fallen dangerously low—only 1,300-1,400 survive today—and continue to fall as their habitat becomes increasingly invaded by ocean debris.[5] Many seals drown from becoming entangled with discarded fishing nets and plastic.[6]

## Fish

In a 2009 study by graduate students from the University of California San Diego, it was discovered that 9.2% of fish living in the convergence zone of the North Pacific Gyre had ingested plastic.

© Ocean Conservancy

© NOAA

© NOAA

Based on this research, it was determined that fish around the Pacific Garbage Patch consume between 12,000-14,000 tons of plastic per year.[7] While more research is required to determine exactly what the effects of ingested micro plastics are on fish and other marine life, the footprint of our consumer waste is apparent.

## Sperm Whales

Recognizable for their large, rounded foreheads, sperm whales are one of eight whales still on the endangered species list.[8] Most sperm whales ingest their food by sucking prey into their mouths, a tactic that makes them extremely vulnerable to ocean debris.[9] In the past few years alone, there have been numerous accounts of beached sperm whales discovered with stomachs full of plastic debris and fishing nets.[1011]

## Laysan Albatross

This large sea bird breeds mostly on the islands of the Central and North Pacific. Albatrosses often times mistake small pieces of plastic for food, which can puncture their intestines or give them a sense of being full without actual nourishment, causing them to slowly starve. Mother albatrosses also often pass plastic particles to their young, whose mortality rates are highest in their first year of life.[1213] While most of the research done on ocean debris' effect on albatrosses has been done on the Laysan Albatross, other species, including the endangered Short-tailed Albatross, are also affected by human consumer waste.[14]

# How can you help?

Join the fight to reduce our footprint on the World's oceans!*

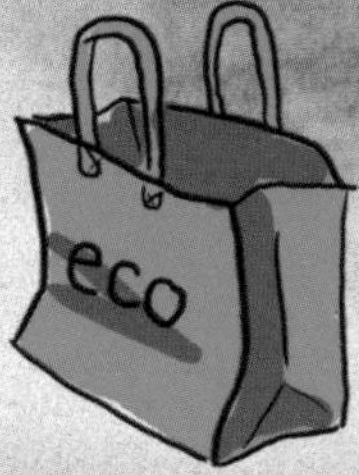

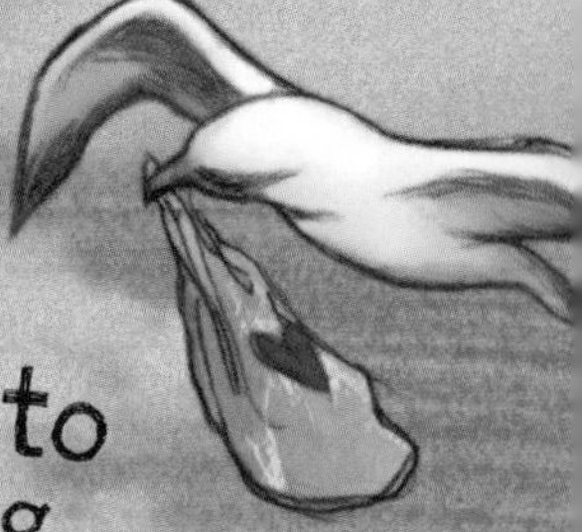

1. Remember to bring along your reusable coffee mug and grocery bags.

2. Check clothing labels and look for products that are made from recycled plastic bottles.

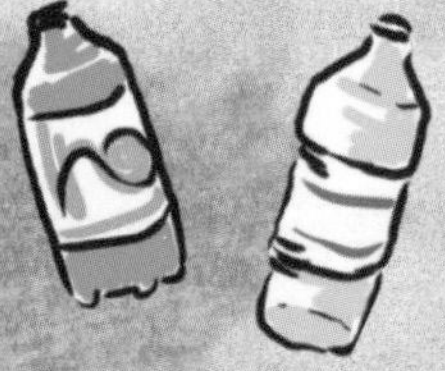

3. Organize a plastic drive in your community.

4. Encourage local businesses to join the EPA's WasteWise initiative to reduce their solid waste.

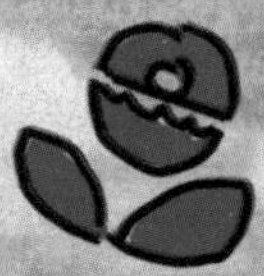

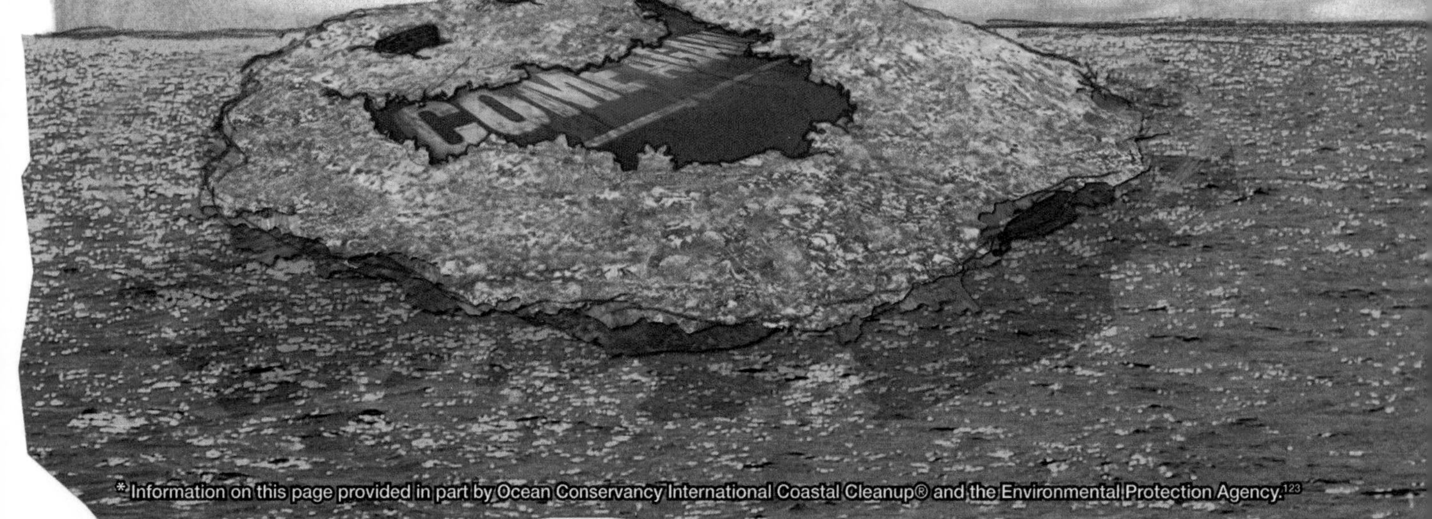

*Information on this page provided in part by Ocean Conservancy International Coastal Cleanup® and the Environmental Protection Agency.[123]

**5.** Contact companies and ask them to reduce packaging and create more environmentally safe products.

**6.** Go the extra mile to always separate your trash items from your recyclables.

**7.** Drink tap water in a reusable water bottle.

**8.** Contribute to fundraising for scientific research to help us better understand the effects of marine debris.

**9.** Buy in bulk as much as possible to reduce the amount of packaging you purchase.

**10.** Write to your legislators and demand policies that address ocean debris.

**11.** Use ashtrays and closable trashcans to keep cigarettes and other garbage from making it into our waterways.

**12.** Volunteer with International Coastal Cleanup® and help clear trash off of our coastlines.

Ocean Conservancy®

© Elyse Butler / Aurora Photos / Ocean Conservancy

**13.** Shop at farmer's markets to reduce the amount of packaging you buy.

**14.** Celebrate Earth Day!

# About the Creator

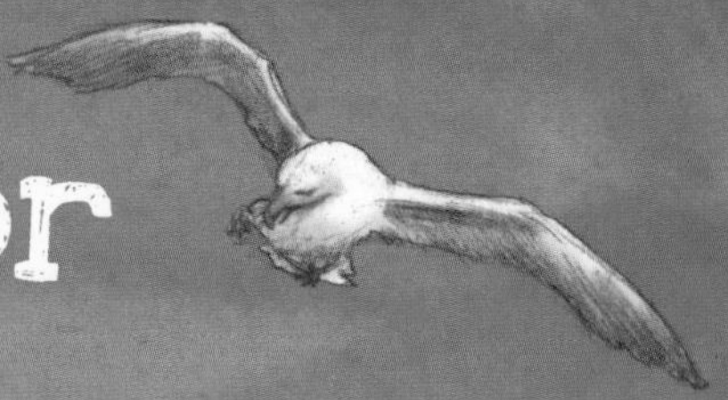

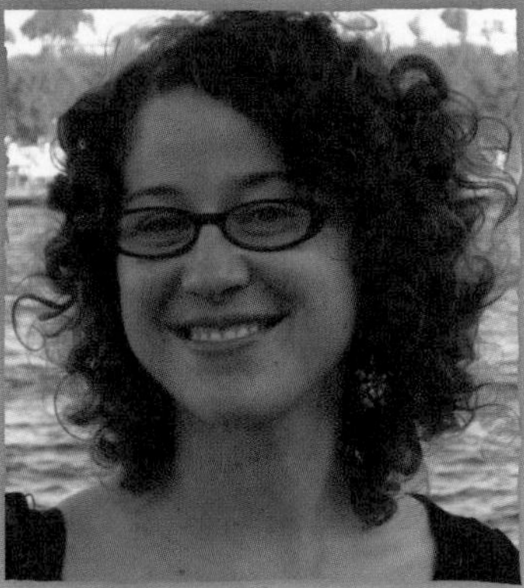

**Rachel Hope Allison** was born and raised in Waco, Texas. Sadly, a lingering "y'all" is all that's left of her Southern drawl, but she has added "dude" to her repertoire after spending ten years in California. She holds an MFA from the School of Visual Arts and a BA from Stanford, and now lives and works in Brooklyn. When she's not drawing, Rachel helps non-profits with their fundraising and communications. In her free time, she runs, reads, and enjoys (generally way too much of) her fiancé Carl's cooking.
**www.rachelhopeallison.com**

## Partners and Contributors

JEFF CORWIN CONNECT™ **JeffCorwinConnect™ Inc.** is a transmedia company co-founded by Jeff Corwin to build a global community of people who care about the future of our planet, and seek to better the world for themselves and their children. JeffCorwinConnect™ is an inclusive community devoted to raising awareness and getting you involved. Find us at **www.facebook.com/jeffcorwinconnect** and get connected!

OceanConservancy® Each year **Ocean Conservancy's International Coastal Cleanup**® brings thousands of people across the world together to work to rid our ocean and waterways of trash, while providing precious data to scientists and researchers. In its first 25 years, more than eight million volunteers have removed 145 million pounds of trash from nearly 300,000 miles. Visit **www.keepthecoastclear.org** to learn more!


**Pages 80-81**

[1] Ocean Conservancy. "The Pacific Garbage Patch: Myths & Realities." 2011. http://www.oceanconservancy.org/our-work/marine-debris/the-pacific-garbage-patch.html

[2] Ocean Conservancy. 2011. http://www.oceanconservancy.org/our-work/marine-debris/international-coastal-cleanup-11.html.

[3] Project Kaisei. 2011. http://www.projectkaisei.org/index.aspx

[4] Ocean Voyage Institute. 2011. http://www.oceanvoyagesinstitute.org/

[5] Fox, Catherine Clark. "Journey to the North Pacific Gyre." Keeping the Coast Clear. 2011. http://www.keepthecoastclear.org/in-the-news/journey-to-the-north-pacific.html

[6] Ocean Conservancy. 2011.

**Pages 82-83**

[1] International Coastal Cleanup/Ocean Conservancy. "Top Ten Items over 25 Years." 2011. http://www.oceanconservancy.org/our-work/marine-debris/assets/images/mdebris_1000_toptenitems25yrsfull_oc.jpg

**Pages 84-85**

[1] U.S. Fish & Wildlife Service. "Loggerhead sea turtle: Caretta caretta." Last modified December 8, 2011. http://ecos.fws.gov/speciesProfile/profile/speciesProfile.action?spcode=C00U

[2] NOAA Fisheries: Office of Protected Resources. "Loggerhead turtle (Caretta caretta)." Last modified September 22, 2011. http://www.nmfs.noaa.gov/pr/species/turtles/loggerhead.htm

[3] NOAA Fisheries: Office of Protected Resources. "Threats to Marine Turtles." Last modified August 15, 2011. http://www.nmfs.noaa.gov/pr/species/turtles/threats.htm

[4] Ocean Conservancy. 2011.

[5] National Geographic. "Hawaiian Monk Seal: Monachus schauinslandi." Accessed December 8, 2011. http://animals.nationalgeographic.com/animals/mammals/hawaiian-monk-seal/

[6] NOAA Marine Debris Program. "De-mystifying the 'Great Pacific Garbage Patch.'" Last modified August 4, 2011. http://marinedebris.noaa.gov/info/patch.html

[7] Davison P, Asch RG (2011) Plastic ingestion by mesopelagic fishes in the North Pacific Subtropical Gyre. Mar Ecol Prog Ser 432:173-180.

[8] U.S. Fish & Wildlife Service. "Endangered Species Program: U.S. Species." Last modified April 7, 2011. http://www.fws.gov/endangered/species/us-species.html

[9] Lambert O, Bianucci G, Post K, de Muizon C, Salas-Gismondi R, Urbina M, Reumer J. (2010) The giant bite of a new raptorial sperm whale from the Miocene epoch of Peru. Nature 466, 105-108 (01 July 2010). doi: 10.1038/nature09067.

[10] Mazzariol S, Di Guardo G, Petrella A, Marsili L, Fossi CM, et al. (2011) Sometimes Sperm Whales (Physeter macrocephalus) Cannot Find Their Way Back to the High Seas: A Multidisciplinary Study on a Mass Stranding. PLoS ONE 6(5): e19417. doi:10.1371/journal.pone.0019417.

[11] Jacobsen J, Massey L, Gulland F. (2010) Fatal ingestion of floating net debris by two sperm whales (Physeter macrocephalus). Marine Pollution Bulletin 60 (2010) 765–767. doi: 10.1016/j.marpolbul.2010.03.008.

[12] Young LC, Vanderlip C, Duffy DC, Afanasyev V, Shaffer SA (2009) Bringing Home the Trash: Do Colony-Based Differences in Foraging Distribution Lead to Increased Plastic Ingestion in Laysan Albatrosses? PLoS ONE 4(10): e7623. doi:10.1371/journal.pone.0007623

[13] Ocean Conservancy. 2011.

[14] U.S. Fish & Wildlife Service. "Endangered and Threatened Wildlife and Plants; Short-Tailed Albatross (Phoebastria albatrus): Initiation of 5-Year Status Review; Availability of Final Recovery Plan." Citation Page 74 FR 23739 23741. 2009. http://ecos.fws.gov/speciesProfile/profile/speciesProfile.action?spcode=B00Y#crithab

**Pages 86-87**

[1] International Coastal Cleanup/Ocean Conservancy. "Ten Things You Can Do For Trash Free Seas." 2011. http://www.oceanconservancy.org/news-room/collateral/images/pressicc_2011report_10things_oceanconservancy.jpg

[2] U.S. Environmental Protection Agency. "Conserving Resources, Preventing Waste." Last modified November 15, 2011. http://www.epa.gov/epawaste/partnerships/wastewise/index.htm

[3] U.S. Environmental Protection Agency. "What You Can Do." Last modified November 15, 2011. http://www.epa.gov/epawaste/wycd/index.htm

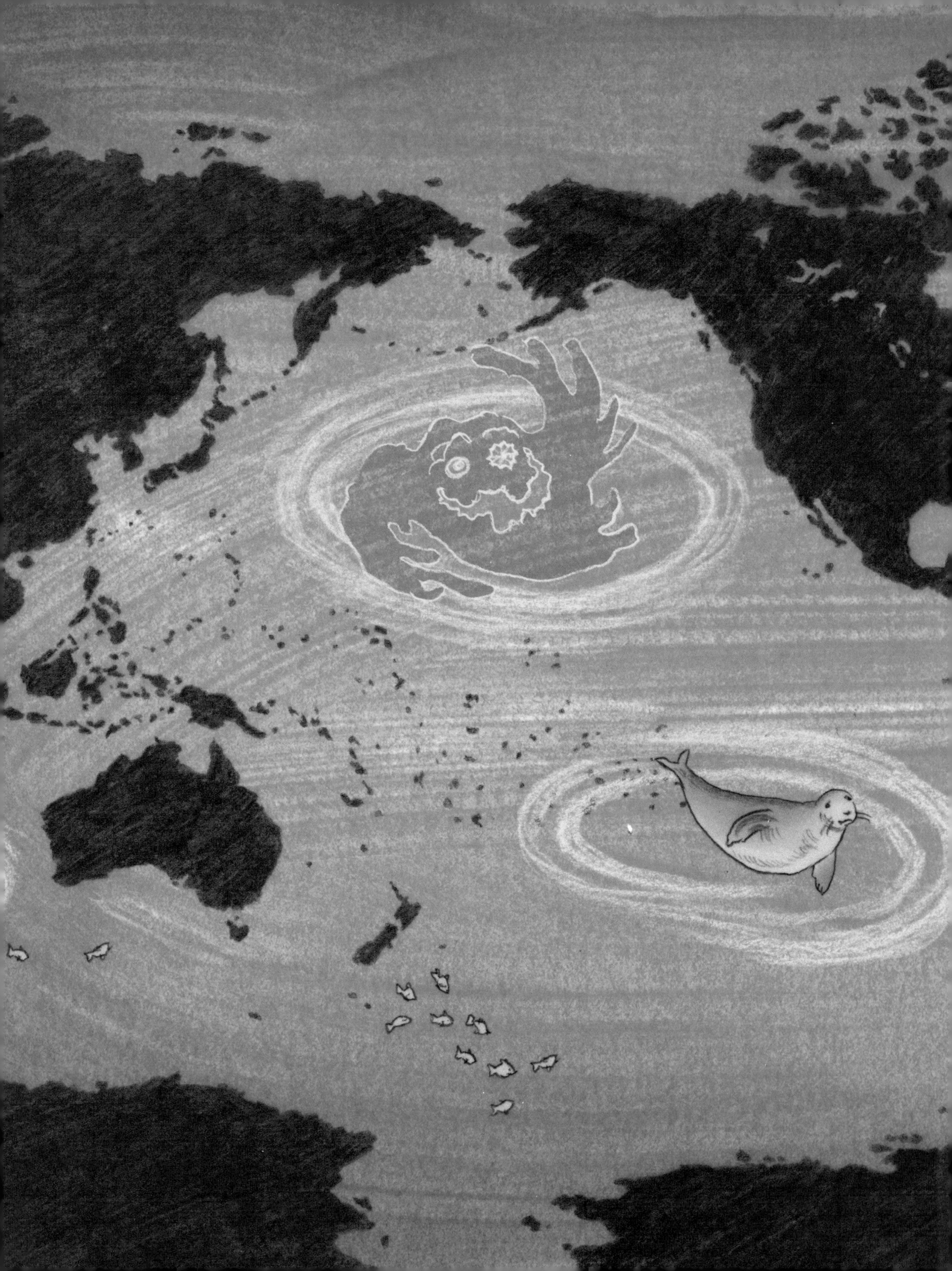